Jean Boisselier

TRENDS IN KHMER ART

Edited by Natasha Eilenberg

Translated by Natasha Eilenberg
and Melvin Elliott

STUDIES ON SOUTHEAST ASIA

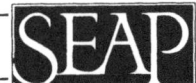

Southeast Asia Program
120 Uris Hall
Cornell University, Ithaca, New York
1989

Originally published as:
Tendances de L'Art Khmèr par
Jean Boisselier
© 1956 Presses Universitaires
de France

CONTENTS

LIST OF ILLUSTRATIONS[1]

---

[1]Letters and figures in parentheses indicate Museum identification.

FOREWORD

The stones of Angkor. For miles around the town of Siem Reap in Kampuchea, pine cone-shaped towers rise above pyramidal platforms and thrust into the heavy skies.. Their forms catch fire and shimmer on the mirrored waters of reservoirs, moats, and canals. Spreading away from them today, as in the past, farmers drive water buffalo over the diked paddy fields, but where the lush green forest is unconstrained, it beats down in waves on the ancient ruins. Looked at from the air, the crisp geometry of the sanctuary ground plans, with their rhythmic ordination of causeways, entrance pavilions, rising terraces, galleries, and towers, is like an immense proposition: a statement both about the order of things, and the ritual machinery to ensure that order, endlessly reaffirming the central fact of origin, the *axis mundi*, where existence touches eternity and the two realms are integrated by a king who, because he participates in divinity, could make life flourish.

These colossal monuments first impressed themselves on the European imagination at the end of the sixteenth century when accounts were written by Spanish and Portuguese visitors. Since that time, any version of the Grand Tour of Asia that failed to include them would be considered incomplete. While there are several very useful books about Khmer art and culture in English, no authoritative guide to the sculpture has been available in an easily accessible paper-bound edition. This book by the distinguished art historian, Jean Boisselier, will remedy that lack. It is a succinct but authoritative introduction to twenty-four of the sculptures housed in the National Museum (formerly Albert-Sarraut Museum) in Phnom Penh. These works were selected by Professor Boisselier, who also prepared the scholarly catalogues of the Museum's collections, and wrote *La statuaire khmère et son évolution*, so that in their ensemble, they give a good representation of the diverse styles developed over many centuries by Khmer artists. Individual works range from the restrained naturalism, athletic grace and blithe repose of the Harihara of Prasat Andèt, a work of the early eighth century, to the precise, hieratic, and almost architectural elegance of the feminine deity in the tenth century Bàkheng style. And in an extraordinary departure from the idealized type forms that characterize Khmer sculpture, there is the deeply poignant portrait statue of what is thought to be Jayavarman VII (1181–circa 1218 A.D.), richly particularized with the marks of time and the force of personality.

Professor Boisselier has drawn on both his prolonged and intimate acquaintance with Khmer art and his keen understanding of the practical problems of the stone carver, to bring out the salient features of these works. At the same time, he lays bare a methodology of stylistic analysis pioneered by Philippe Stern and subsequently elaborated and practiced with great success by several generations of scholars of the *Ecole française d'Extrême-Orient*. In this, a number of elements or motifs are first isolated and then assembled into sequences, often, but by no means always, following a gradual pattern of innovation or development out of a background of shared conventions. Ultimately, these elements are brought into mutual presence, and also with epigraphy, so that a system of concomitances may be discerned and a chronology, either relative or absolute, established. The styles, as Professor Boisselier points out, are designated by the names of architectural monuments that exhibit the most characteristic elements of their period.

All of the sculptures discussed here are drawn from the world of the court and monastery, and thus they are part of a tradition of learning including city planning, political terminology and thought, religious ritual and systems of writing, that links India and Southeast Asia in a great cultural *oikoumene*. This integration of the princely courts of Southeast Asia into classical Indian culture, apparently took place as early as the first centuries A.D. but not everywhere, nor all at once, and there is evidence of even earlier contacts in the late centuries B.C. It is not clear either why these exchanges across political, cultural, and ecological frontiers bore such fruit when they did, or whether Indian models were actually formative in the development of civilization in Southeast Asia or whether Southeast Asians merely found in them a framework to construe already existing and parallel forms of life.

As might be expected, a great deal of scholarly labor has been expended on unraveling the causal nexus of this conjoining of imaginations across great distances. At one time or another emphasis has been placed on either colonization or trade, with the principal actors being either Indian princely adventurers or merchants. In these explanations, primacy of initiative is on the Indian side of the equation, and the process is characterized by such causal simplicities as influence and response, source and imitation.

With, however, the relatively recent growth of a historiography that seeks to account for developments in Southeast Asia by a scrutiny of institutional patterns, social forces, and cultural movements within the region itself, there is a tendency to place the initiative for selective borrowing squarely on the side of emerging elites within Southeast Asia. In this variant, local chiefs sought to avail themselves of the consecration rituals, higher-order political models and theory, as well as the universalizing characteristics of Indian religions and philosophical speculation. Indian brahmins would thus have served in much the same way as the steady stream of experts that move about the world today bringing useful scientific and technical skills to agrarian societies in the process of modernization.

In the end, all of the above explanations may be found to be partially true. We may very well find that the variety of themes, motives, and forms that Southeast Asians shared with those living on the Indian subcontinent were parallel responses to the breakup of the world of late prehistory. That cosmos of particular place, of village, family, tribe, ancestors, and tutelary deities, a bounded but dynamic world, had burst its confining order in the last centuries B.C. Certainly not everywhere, but at some strategic and exposed places, it lay in fragments, the old coherence shattered by the experience of social inequalities and distances, the confusing patterns of urban scale, the cosmopolitan flux of goods and ideas in extended trading networks, all of this contributing to the loss of the certainties that link past, present, and future to the measure of a human fate. In these altered circumstances, through a myriad of connections, the central themes, the imaginative forms, of a world on the wane were restated in the only cultural patterns at hand that claimed to be universal: the classical tradition of the Indian courts.

By parallel, analogy, consonance, a system of equivalents was developed in which, for example, elaborate local death customs to effect the transformation and release of the soul, could be restated within the frame of Hindu *śraddha* rites. Khmer chieftains living on scattered estates ringed by hostile enemies and deep forests, engaged in a struggle for spoils, slaves, and women, could come to see their lives reflected and magnified in the ideal frame of the great Indian epics, the *Mahābhārata* and the *Rāmāyana*. They could "read" themselves and their lives in the polished behavior, the exalted passions, the stern face of duty figured in the epics. Their familiar and potent landscape, too, was folded into the glamor and radiance of the epics. Their own sacred springs and bathing places became *tirtha* (fords or crossing places from the mundane to the divine world), their sacred mountains where the ancestors were venerated became Śiva's mountain above. Indra's divine kingship became a metaphor by which men of local prominence could exalt their claims to authority, and the Hindu cosmogony with its system of *yuga*, or progressive cycle of epochs, could provide local space and secular time with a supernatural design. By such "localizations" these universal imported traditions of India were fitted to the varying ecological circumstances, pre-existent traditions, and daily round of life in the multicentric world of Southeast Asia.

The earliest sculptures discussed in this book, those predating the ninth century, mark the seed-time of the first Khmer supravillage political systems. Because they are public statements, they inevitably have a political significance and are inseparable from the process of state formation. The sculptures and the temples that enframe them express both universal religious values and a local ancestral piety: they also make that piety possible, visible and powerful. In this way they can be seen to reinforce the preeminence of local elites. After the ninth century, when a state cult was inaugurated with appropriate consecration rituals, sculpture becomes part of a great system of correspondences and analogies that underwrite and elaborate Khmer political and social order. In the thirteenth century during the reign of Jayavarman VII, this culminates in a veritable forest of symbols finding its ultimate expression in the baroque, face-towers of his temple-mountain, the Bàyon.

The English translation of Professor Boisselier's French text is the work of Mrs. Natasha Eilenberg and Melvin Elliott. Mrs. Eilenberg edited the present edition, provided a glossary, map, pen drawings, and a chronological chart which will add much to the usefulness of this volume. Her careful and devoted efforts are a measure of her high regard for Professor Boisselier, her teacher and friend of many years.

Stanley J. O'Connor

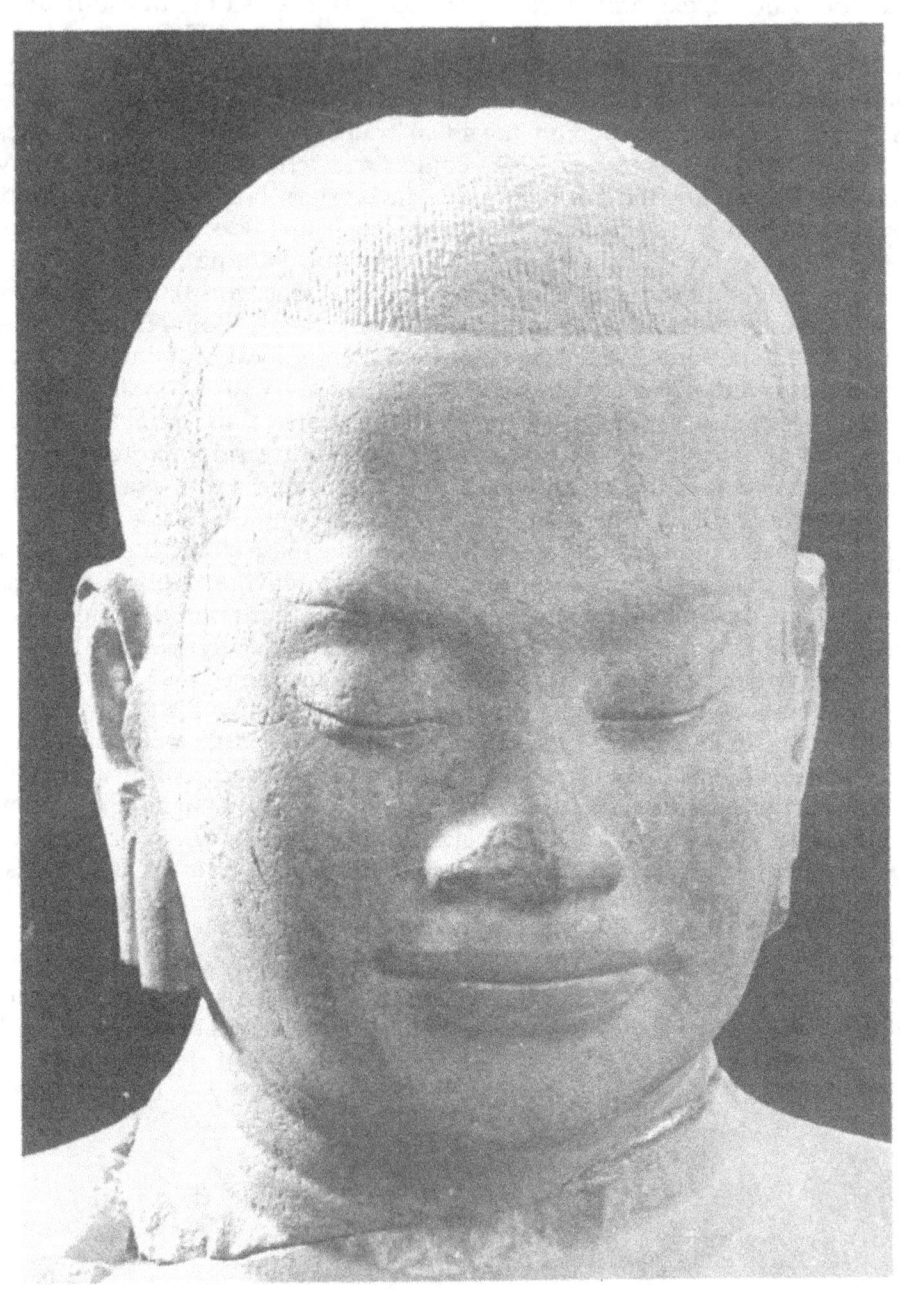

Jayavarman VII (?) (Detail of the head)
cf. Figure XIX, page 82

PREFACE TO THE ENGLISH TRANSLATION

This English translation of the *Tendances de l'art khmer* is quite different from the work written in 1952 and published in Paris in 1956 (*Bibliothèque de Diffusion du Musée Guimet, Tome LXII*). It is also more extensive than the Japanese edition published in Tokyo in 1984. While both the Japanese version and this translation include the same reassessments of iconographic data dictated by recent studies and our own continued research, and update an obsolete bibliography, this edition has been further enriched. At the instigation of our translator and friend Mrs. Natasha Eilenberg, and thanks to her help, it has acquired a number of addenda. Their purpose is to make the *Tendances* more accessible to readers who have not necessarily studied the history of Khmer art and who are not familiar with a terminology gradually developed by French scholars in the last sixty or so years.

In its original form, the work as we conceived it was first of all intended for art lovers, visitors to the Phnom Penh Museum, students of Khmer art, as well as for a public somewhat aware of the problems raised and familiar with a methodology stemming from the early works of Philippe Stern (1927). Still, we tried "to avoid excessive technical terms and forbidding erudition." Today, conditions are altogether different from what they were when we wrote the *Tendances de l'art khmer*. Very few can now go to the site of Angkor or visit the Phnom Penh Museum. And although interest in Khmer art has never really been lost, in the past twenty years access to it has become more difficult. These are the reasons why we heeded Mrs. Eilenberg's suggestions and accepted her enrichment of our brief work with the addition of a glossary, a chronological chart, of pen drawings, and a map. All these, she believed, would increase the didactic impact of the work.

We wish to take this opportunity to thank her for the extreme care she has taken with our text as well as for her constant concern to bring it within easy reach of its future readers. Our thanks also go to Mr. Melvin Elliott who has assisted her in her translation, and to Professor Stanley J. O'Connor whose kind words in his masterful and scholarly Foreword have deeply touched us. Finally, and we cannot emphasize it enough, we are highly honored by the welcome the Southeast Asia Program of Cornell University afforded the modest work that was solely inspired by the beauty and the diversity of Khmer statuary.

Paris, 1989
Jean Boisselier

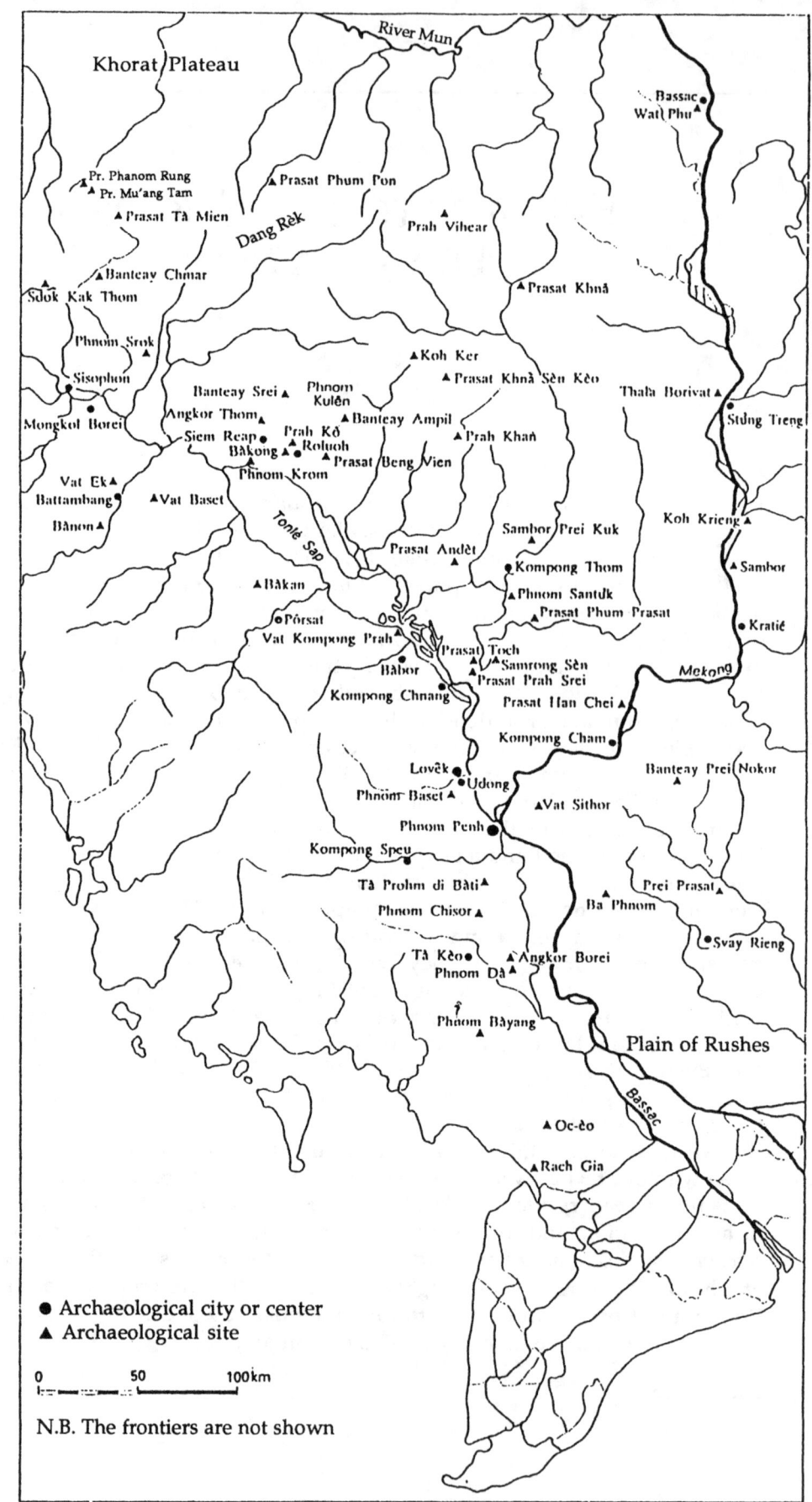

MAP OF CAMBODIA

INTRODUCTION

The objective of this brief work is simply to present and describe twenty-four sculptures chosen from among the most representative of Khmer art. These statues are examples with outstanding aesthetic qualities that most succinctly demonstrate the evolution of Khmer statuary over some ten centuries. All of the pieces belong to the collections of the Phnom Penh National Museum. If some periods may seem illustrated more abundantly than others, it is only because they were especially brilliant.

At this time, we believe it useful to offer all art lovers not necessarily versed in archaeology an overall picture of the evolution of Khmer statuary with emphasis on its strong originality and vitality. We do this without waiting for the publication of our catalogues which have been years in preparation and are meant mainly for the scientific community. We have tried to avoid excessive technical terms and forbidding erudition for those who seek only the emotional gift of art, but we believe it is essential to present each work in the light of our latest research.

The styles we refer to are named after the monuments that best characterize Khmer art during the major periods of its history. However, it would be unwise to consider these periods as an aribitrary division, with each monument standing alone in a vacuum, without ties or relation with the ones surrounding it. Art is a living thing, and a reflection of life itself. Styles are only convenient landmarks; just as in French art, where the Louis XV style does not succeed the Louis XIV style without keeping attributes of it, so for instance, the Prah Kô style (last quarter of the IXth century), does not follow the Kulên style (first half of the IXth century), with the sudden changes occasionally encountered in biological mutations. Whichever period it may belong to, the final stages of a style invariably show the signs of the major trends which will be the hallmarks of the new style. And the new style, at least in its beginning, will retain some carryover from the period that preceded it.

We feel it is necessary to include these remarks so that some readers are not confused by a terminology whose principles were offered by our teacher Phillippe Stern some 59 years ago and have since been followed with great success.

Phnom Penh, January–March 1953

Text and Bibliography revised and updated, Paris 1986

N.B. A short list of readily understood and fairly easily available works appears on p. 117. For more exhaustive research the reader will benefit from the publications of the *Bulletin de l'Ecole française d'Extrême-Orient*, the *Bulletin de la*

Commission archéologique de l'Indochine, the *Journal Asiatique*, the *Revue des Arts Asiatiques*, of *Artibus Asiae*, the *Bulletin de la Société des Etudes indochinoises*, the *Cahiers de l'Ecole française d'Extrême-Orient*, ... etc.

All the works which appeared before 1927 give an erroneous chronology which was based on the wrong interpretation of inscriptions, giving the end of the IXth century as the date for the Bàyon. Its correct date, about 1200, was only determined thanks to the works of Ph. Stern, G. Cœdès, and V. Goloubew; the first of these authors showed that it was impossible to accept the previously admitted chronology, the next one returned the Bàyon to its builder Jayavarman VII, and the last identified the IXth century shrine mentioned in the Phnom Bàkheng inscription. Nevertheless, errors still exist in some works which appeared after 1927, and essential references will be additionally provided by the following works: for history, *Indianized States of Southeast Asia* (Honolulu, 1968) of G. Cœdès; for art, *L'Art Khmer, Les grandes étapes* ... of G. de Coral-Rémusat and for the statuary, the works of Pierre Dupont and of the author.

THE HISTORY

Cambodia received its culture from India like the whole of Southeast Asia, but other than rather scanty epigraphy, the earliest documents we have concerning the very first centuries of Cambodia's history are the narratives of Chinese envoys. Their critical discrimination, however, is not always evident, and their judgement is often subject to considerable national pride. . . . Be that as it may, they left us a collection of very valuable documents for the study of Cambodia from the IIIrd century on.

The Chinese narratives reveal two successive waves of Indianization[1] superimposed on an original civilization whose importance is far from negligible. Continuous maritime connections with the West introduced other influences alongside the essential Indian contribution: Roman, Hellenistic, and Iranian. These are evidenced by the remarkable discoveries made in the 1940s by Louis Malleret who later became Director of the *Ecole française d'Extrême-Orient* (French School of Far Eastern Studies), on the site of Oc-èo in the Trans-Bassac (south of present-day Viêt Nam, to the southwest of the Mekong Delta).

Until the VIth century the future Cambodia was divided into two kingdoms: the Funan and Zhenla of the Chinese historians. Funan, a maritime confederation of the Gulf of Thailand embracing the south of present-day Viêt Nam and the south of present-day Cambodia, exercised its suzerainty over Zhenla, a continental state that included northern Cambodia, a portion of Laos and of the Khorat plateau.

---

[1]Properly speaking, the Indianization of Southeast Asia was not a colonization resulting from military conquests, but an expansion of Indian civilization favored by commercial navigation.

While there is evidence today that contacts between India and Southeast Asia date back to the IVth–Vth centuries B.C., the notion of the two so-called waves of Indianization was essentially based on Chinese sources which attributed the two waves to the arrival in Southeast Asia of two personages named Kaundinya, mentioned some three or four centuries apart.

First, there is the legend of Kaundinya, a Brahman who came in the Ist century A.D. and founded the kingdom of Funan. Historical personalities are known in the IInd century A.D.; in the 1st half of the IIIrd century the Chinese established contacts with Funan, and the four oldest Sanskrit inscriptions date from that period.

Then, in the 2nd half of the IVth century A.D., the Chinese Annals mention the reign of "Chandan," and a Kiao-tch'en-jou (Kaundinya), one of his successors who came by way of the Malay Peninsula. Marked by a recrudescence of Indianization, the end of the IVth and the Vth centuries, according to G. Cœdès, would correspond to the 2nd wave of Indianization. In fact, as evidenced by the epigraphy, the more or less pronounced influence of newly arrived Brahmans from India appears throughout the history, to say nothing of the times of Jayavarman VII when, following the conquests made by Islam, Buddhist priests sought refuge in Southeast Asia. (J.B./Ed.)

During the VIth century the sovereigns of Zhenla progressively increased their strength at Funan's expense, and finally seized it towards the middle of the century. The birth of the Khmer kingdom resulted from the unification of the two kingdoms to the benefit of Zhenla. It was consecrated in the first half of the VIIth century by the founding of Īśānapura, the capital of Īśānavarman (Sambor Prei Kuk in Kompong Thom province). This founding seems to mark, at least in the artistic field, the decline of Indian influences. It is also the time when, forsaking the maritime contacts of ancient Funan, Khmer civilization turned to land-based interests.

At first, the unification of the two early kingdoms was short-lived; by the end of the century the new kingdom was divided again into two rival states: Land (or Upper) Zhenla and Water (or Lower) Zhenla. The latter was no doubt attempting to recover part of Funan's lost autonomy and sea power. The rivalry was such that it eventually led to a state of semi-anarchy which continued throughout the VIIIth century, if not longer. This weakened state seems to have been exploited by several feudal principalities in an effort to gain their own emancipation. Mostly, however, the political chaos served the designs of Java which, in an undertaking directed against all of the central and eastern portions of the Malay Peninsula, Champa, and even Việt Nam, managed to impose its suzerainty over Cambodia for some time.

The liberation and the lasting unification of the land were the achievement, though probably indirect, of Jayavarman II who seems to have been held a captive of Java in his youth. In the course of a reign which began early in the IXth century and spanned some fifty years, this monarch progressively established his authority, if not over all of Cambodia, at least over the northern region of the Lakes, the true cradle of Khmer power. The initiation of the royal Śivaite cult of the Devarāja or God-king on Mount Mahendra (present-day Phnom Kulên), secured the foundations of the Angkorian monarchy upon solid religious bases. Jayavarman II was an itinerant king; eventually he returned to Hariharalaya (near Rolûoh), a capital he had founded in the early stages of his reign, where he died. His first successors resided there, and before the end of the IXth century, Yaśovarman I, the builder of the first Angkor, also came from there. Yaśodharapura, the site he chose and which the succeeding monarchs seldom left during four centuries, is named after him. It should not be confused with Angkor Thom, enclosed within high walls, which was not built until the end of the XIIth century, and centered on the Bàyon. Yaśodharapura was a larger town, situated a little more to the southwest, with Phnom Bàkheng as its geometric and religious center. The moats and the levees of the old city can still be seen along nearly half their length.

Soon after the reign of Yaśovarman I the new capital was abandoned, though not for very long. Jayavarman IV, Yaśovarman's almost immediate successor, moved the court to Chok Gargyar (present-day Koh Ker) but only remained there from 921 until 944. The sovereigns returned then and settled more or less permanently on the site Yaśovarman had selected, not within the enclosure he probably had traced, but in its immediate vicinity. From then on, all the great royal institutions arose there: the eastern Mébon and Pré Rup in the second half of the Xth century, the Royal Palace and Tà Kev near the very end of the same century, the Bàphuon in the XIth century, and finally, in about 1100–1150, Angkor Vat: uncontested masterpiece of Khmer architecture and symbol of Sūryavarman II's might.

In 1177 Angkor, the capital, was taken by surprise and occupied by the armies of Champa, an ancient kingdom located in the center of Viêt Nam, and like Cambodia also Indianized. There again, after driving out the invader, king Jayavarman VII rebuilt the royal city of Angkor Thom centered on the Bàyon and "clothed in her ramparts." So read the inscriptions extolling her single wall, twelve kilometers long with five monumental gateways. In the course of a reign that lasted from 1181 until perhaps 1219, this monarch lifted Khmer glory to its highest point, extended the boundaries of the kingdom to their farthest limits, enhanced it throughout with prestigious religious monuments, and gave it a whole network of utilitarian and charitable institutions: irrigation basins, roads, bridges, rest houses, and hospitals. Jayavarman VII was the last great monarch who sponsored major constructions. Despite the decline that began to show soon after his death, in 1296 Angkor was still brilliant enough to fill the Chinese envoy Zhou Daguan with an admiration which inspired his dazzling description of the city.

Under the growing advance of the young Thai kingdom of Ayuthya, the ancient capital had to be abandoned shortly before the middle of the XVth century. The center of the kingdom was moved further south towards less vulnerable areas, and finally settled at the junction of the *Quatre Bras*, on the site of Phnom Penh.[1]

Angkor was never forgotten, but nonetheless gradually came under Thai domination, and was not returned to Cambodia until 1907. Cutting through the brush, consolidating the monuments stone by stone, the *Ecole française d'Extrême-Orient* then gave her back some of her past glory and, through a judicious study of epigraphic texts, retraced a history that had bowed out to legend.

---

[1]The junction of the Four Arms, i.e., of the Mekong and the outflow of the Great Lakes. [Ed.]

THE RELIGIONS

Khmer art is an almost entirely religious art where even utilitarian structures such as bridges and basins come under divine protection.

Hinduism and Buddhism, the two great religions that belong to Indian culture, were practiced in ancient Cambodia. Both are founded on the principle of the transmigration of beings, from birth to rebirths, and on the pursuit of the proper means to free them from this cycle.

Hinduism gathers an extraordinarily rich pantheon around a divine trinity made up of Brahmā, Vishnu, and Śiva. In the course of its history the religion has greatly evolved.

Theoretically, Brahmā is the supreme god, but he never plays more than a secondary role. He is depicted with four heads and four arms.

Vishnu, the Protector and Savior of the worlds, like Śiva has numerous sectarian followers. He has only one head, and most often four arms. Between each cosmic period he lies asleep on the Serpent of Eternity while the future world is being formed. As eternal Savior, he appears in a new form, animal or human, at each of his awakenings. These *avatāra* were often shown by the sculptors; the most popular ones are undoubtedly those of Rāma, the hero of the Rāmāyana (Cambodian version Reamker), and of Krishna, the seductive shepherd and charmer endowed with prodigious strength.

Śiva is the Creator, Keeper, and Destroyer of the Worlds. He has one or five heads, and two or multiple arms. His forehead generally bears a third vertical eye and his hair, usually gathered up in a high chignon, is adorned with the lunar crescent. Śiva is represented in the aspects evocative of the various roles he can play, and is often shown in the symbolic form of the *linga*, this being especially true of Khmer art.

Next to these divinities appear their energies represented in a feminine form which often causes them to be considered as their "spouses." They are the *śakti:* Śrī, Lakshmī, for Vishnu; Pārvatī, Umā, Durgā, Kālī, etc., for Śiva; their forms being kind or terrifying depending on whether they represent protective or destructive forces.

Among the divinities of the Hindu pantheon most often depicted we must also mention Ganeśa, Śiva's son, god of intelligence and of knowledge endowed with the head of an elephant; Skanda, another son of Śiva, is the War-god; Indra, the former supreme god who commands the thunder and the rains, has only retained primacy among the secondary gods; Sūrya is the sun-god.

The divinities' mounts (*vāhana*) likewise, have an important role: Brahmā's *vāhana* is Hamsa, the sacred goose; that of Vishnu is the fabulous bird Garuda, and Śiva's is the bull Nandin. Indra is carried by the three-headed elephant

Airavāta, Skanda by a peacock, and Sūrya rides a chariot. In order to complete the list we would still have to cite a multitude of deities who often only play a retiring role in Khmer art, plus a host of demi-gods, heroes, and nymphs who have held such an important place in the decoration of the temples: *deva* and *devatā*, *yaksha*, *asura*, *apsaras*, *nāga* and *nāgī*.

Buddhism brings to all the possibility of liberation through the example and the teaching of the Buddha. Very early, the doctrine inspired two major sects: the first, which today is called Theravāda (the Doctrine of the Elders), uses the Pāli Canon, and is practiced in Sri Lanka and in most of the Indochinese Peninsula, or the Sanskrit language (it is then called Hīnayāna, the "Small Vehicle"). The other is the Mahāyāna (the "Great Vehicle"), the Buddhism of the North (Nepal, Tibet, China, Korea, Japan). The Theravāda is agnostic in its essential meaning and only offers the example and the image of the Buddha for the edification of the faithful. But in developing the philosophical aspect of the teaching, conversely, the "Great Vehicle" brings the historical Buddha into a very complex pantheon of Bodhisattvas or future Buddhas, and of Dhyāni-Buddhas or Contemplative Buddhas, and assimilates the majority of Hindu divinities although it mostly keeps them in the background.

Inscriptions show that both Hinduism and Hīnayāna Buddhism were practiced in Cambodia in the first centuries of its history. This form of Buddhism used the Sanskrit language, whereas Theravāda Buddhism practiced today uses Pāli. It would seem that Mahāyāna began to spread only in the VIIth and the VIIIth centuries. In the IXth century the initiation of the Devarāja ritual increased the importance of Śivaism and brought on a Buddhist retreat, although mostly official. If Buddhism slumbered then for a few centuries, though in a perfectly tolerant state, the same cannot be said of Vishnuism which always retained a considerable importance, attested by the number of images and the importance of its monuments. Towards the middle of the Xth century, Buddhism of the Mahāyāna doctrine timidly rose again. Vishnuism became especially predominant under Sūrya-varman II who built the immense Angkor Vat temple for Vishnu with whom he identified himself in death. The religious fervor of Jayavarman VII, and his strong personality brought on the triumph of the Mahāyāna for a relatively short period that led to an extraordinary flowering of monuments. But the triumph was short-lived for probably soon after his reign a Śivaite reaction occurred, intolerant and iconoclastic, and exceptional in Khmer History. . . . Buddhism, meanwhile, pursued its own course; it asserted itself permanently, but in the Pāli language Theravāda form which came through contacts with Sri Lanka, no later than the end of the XIIIth century.

While Khmer images are ruled by the imperatives of iconographic data received from India, they display their own set of characteristics. Hinduism in Cambodia has always backed away from the ferocious, the erotic, or the macabre aspects in which India so often indulged.

Vishnu is mostly represented with four arms, holding the mace, the conch, the *cakra* (a disc or rather a wheel-shaped weapon), and a ball that represents the Earth and replaces India's lotus bud. Less frequently in statuary, and especially in the early period and in the XIIth century, he appears in some of his *avatāra*.

Śiva generally has only one head and two arms, but in his Sadāśiva aspect (ever benevolent), he can have five heads and ten arms. Depictions of the Tandava or cosmic dance are exceptional; those showing him in the form of the *liṅga* occur most frequently.

Śiva can also be joined with Vishnu in the form of Harihara, a hybrid divinity whose right half is made in his image and the left half is in the likeness of Vishnu. This divinity was known in India, but was even more popular in Cambodia.

In Buddhist imagery, the Buddha wears the monastic garb, and is often adorned with jewelry; he even has a diadem. For the most part he is depicted seated on the coils of the seven-headed Nāgarāja who protects his meditation with his unfolded hood. While the *mudrā* or gestures the Buddha performs are, of course, those of Indian iconography, it should be noted that the Teaching gesture is unknown.

Amidst the Mahāyānist pantheon, images of Lokeśvara, the compassionate Bodhisattva, and of Prajñāpāramitā, the "perfection of Wisdom" or of Tārā, the "Savioress," are by far the most numerous. All are dressed like the Hindu divinities, but in front of the chignon they bear the small figure of a seated meditating Buddha.

Lokeśvara is preferably depicted with four arms, holding the flask, the book, the rosary, and the lotus bud. But he may also have eight arms. In the art of Jayavarman VII his torso, even his hair are sometimes covered then with a multitude of small Buddha images and of divinities which the Bodhisattva is meant to irradiate for the salvation of beings. Generally in stone sculptures in the round, Tārā only has two arms and holds the book and the lotus bud or two lotus buds.

Tantric divinities with multiple arms and heads appear very rarely in great sculpture in the true sense of the word, but bronzes and some steles show a number of beautiful examples of these iconographic forms.

We hope that these very briefly summarized basics will help art lovers identify the divinities most often depicted in Khmer statuary, though it must also be emphasized that very often bronzes reveal aspects far more complex than the ones illustrated in stone.

THE STATUARY

The fine qualities and the originality of Khmer statuary were noted very early. In 1875 the Comte de Croizier wrote:

The Khmers brought their statuary to a high degree of perfection. The types they depict are indigenous types: the faces have a smiling and gentle expression, their general character is hieratic. Even when the figures are in motion their muscular forms are not brought out. . . . Their works have undeniable originality, and it is impossible to mistake the statues from India for the ones found in the ancient temples of Cambodia.

A genuine interest, however, did not begin to appear until 1910 when the first scientific catalogs of G. Cœdès and H. Parmentier were published, and especially after the so-called "Commaille" Buddha was found in 1913 and named after its discoverer, the first Curator of the Angkor Monuments. In the very year of its discovery, the plastic qualities and the highly classical beauty of the work were underscored in the authoritative writings of Alfred Foucher.

Although the merits and the diversity of the statuary were recognized, dating, or even a relative chronology were practically unknown. While in some particularly fortunate instances inscriptions can reveal the date of monuments, this does not apply to statues which are very rarely inscribed. Moreover, their frequently repeated consecrations and inherently mobile character stand in the way of safely ascribing to them the date of the monument that shelters them.

Thanks to a number of rather clear characteristics brought to light by the labors of H. Parmentier, G. Cœdès, and Paul Bellugue, the earliest statues predating the IXth century could soon be isolated. The rest of the statuary, representing the artistic activity of some four centuries, remained grouped under the vague designation of "Angkorian" because broadly it corresponded to the Angkor period. It was actually made up of greatly varied elements where only the statuary of the Koh Ker group, which is rather well defined in time and space, could provide a chronological reference. Philippe Stern, the former Head Curator of the Musée Guimet, has the exceptional merit of being the first to recognize the evolution of Khmer sculpture. Back in 1927 he presented a method for the study of Khmer art. Using this method and further developing it, Pierre Dupont and Gilberte de Coral-Rémusat defined the first results. Broadening Philippe Stern's research, we, in turn, were able to throw light on the last obscure points, and we believe that today we can show the continuous evolution of Khmer statuary from approximately the VIth century until the abandonment of Angkor.

This evolution seems to be marked by two polarities of almost opposite ideals. One takes place in the very first centuries, the other corresponds to the reign of Jayavarman VII and the so-called art "of the Bàyon." In the interim, at times the art leaned more to naturalism, at others to hieratical forms; it tended to be more gentle or more austere.

If we accept the testimony of the Chinese texts, and of archaeological finds which, so far, have yielded no stone work that can be dated earlier than the middle of the VIth century, the statuary does not seem to appear until almost the very end of Funan where only metal casting and wood carving may have been practiced for a long time. After Funan disappeared under Zhenla's hegemony, the statuary upheld the traditions of the earliest ateliers with a clearer trend towards naturalism. When the secession of the two Zhenlas occurred towards the end of the VIIth century, the state of semi-anarchy which prevailed in most of the country brought on in certain regions a rapid decadence. This seems to be reflected in the clumsy copying of earlier models, and an often disconcerting technical ignorance. And yet, some centers of ancient Zhenla retained all of their vitality, and produced some truly remarkable masterpieces.

The reign of Jayavarman II seems to indicate a renovative effort in every domain. A new aesthetic, less naturalistic but also more majestic, which had appeared in the Kulên monuments, fully bloomed in the Rolûoh group in the last quarter of the IXth century. The founding of Angkor showed the triumph of hieratic trends with powerful forms, much more architectural than lifelike. The reign of Jayavarman IV at Koh Ker continued this trend, but it also showed the paradox of an astonishing preference for dynamism, so surprising in Khmer art. A few years after the abandonment of Koh Ker, the endowment in 967 of a temple by a major religious dignitary at Banteay Srei, some 30 kilometers from Angkor, brought into fashion an all-gentle art that borrowed from the styles of the VIIth and VIIIth centuries, and also from the art of Java. The XIth century persevered along the same lines; absorbing and assimilating the innovations of Banteay Srei, it inclined towards simplicity and sought a graceful slenderness. The first half of the XIIth century, however, broke away from this ideal. The art of the Angkor Vat style, more decorative than naturalistic, returned to hieratic forms, and bedecked its statues with jewelry and finely sculptured diadems.

The reign of Jayavarman VII marked a new and radical change: animated by the Buddhist ideal, the statuary shed its fineries and was lit up by a mystic smile vibrating with interior life. The œuvre then counted only for the facial expression and the gesture of the hands. But another trend was also reflected in the art of Jayavarman VII, which was new in Khmer art, in that it sought to achieve true portraiture. Until then the statuary was impersonal, but in a complex feeling that somewhat recalls the Amarnian reaction of Egyptian art,[1] it then tended to model itself on the image of the royal family. In the best of the works, this determination

---

[1]After Tell el'Amarna or Tell Amarna, on the East bank of the Nile in Egypt. Site of Akhenaton, the ancient capital of King Amenhotep IV (ca. 1375–ca. 1358 B.C.). After the 4th year of his reign he undertook a complete reform in an effort to unify political, social, and artistic life under a monotheistic system. Opposed by the clergy, he broke off with it and changed his name to Akhenaton. Under his direct influence his art was characterized by true portraiture to such an extent that even the models' physical flaws were represented. His period was one of the greatest of Egyptian art. The busts of his queen Nefertiti are examples of it. (Ed.)

led to a quest for anatomical truth, and a sincerity long disavowed by Khmer artists.[1]

Beginning with the latter part of the XIIIth century, influences from the art of the Mae Nam Basin in the west made themselves felt by modifying the facial expressions and the pattern of adornment. Thai aesthetic was soon to impose its conceptions. But the radiance of Khmer art remained such that when the Siamese artists made Hindu idols in the height of the XVIth century, they still copied almost slavishly the old Khmer models.

The Musée Albert-Sarraut was founded in 1920 at the instigation of George Groslier, who personally took over the somewhat ill-assorted bases of the Musée Khmer de Phnom Penh. The Musée Khmer had been created under the auspices of the *Ecole française d'Extrême-Orient* in order to protect works scattered throughout the provinces of the kingdom. The Musée Albert-Sarraut, now the Musée National, houses the world's largest collection of Khmer statues. But in 1949, when the writer was appointed its Curator, there were still serious gaps; some periods were not represented at all or they were only illustrated by mediocre works. We have endeavored to remedy this inadequacy by transferring pieces from the archaeological stores of Angkor, by conducting prospecting missions, and by establishing a modern presentation program. The Musée National has in its collections not only the most authoritative masterpieces for the enjoyment of art lovers, but thanks to an exceptionally valuable documentation, it also offers researchers and scholars alike the possibility of studying Khmer art in its entirety.

---

[1] It should be noted that the notion of copying, of seeking formal similarity, is foreign to Indianized arts. Various styles prescribe canons which only entail a relative resemblance. Even when dealing with the exceptional case of the three Vishnus from Prasat Damrei Krap (Phnom Kulên), which are most likely the works of the same sculptor, we have three statues which are very close, but by no means alike. (On this subject, cf. A. B. Griswold, "Imported Images and the Nature of Copying in the Art of Siam," in *Essays Offered to G. H. Luce*, Artibus Asiae Publishers, Ascona 1966, Vol. II, pp. 37–73.)

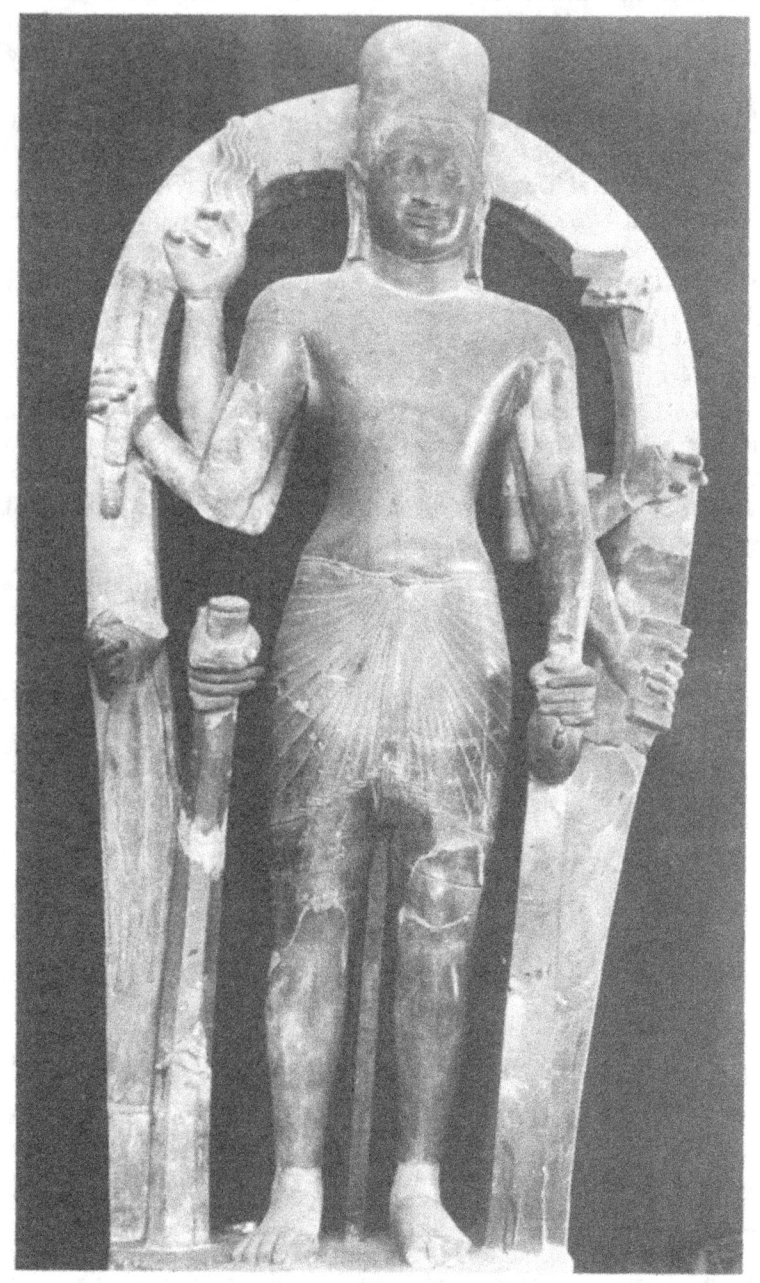

FIGURE I

FIGURE I

Vishnu (B-30, 18)
Schist (H. 2m. 70—106 5/16"), Phnom Dà (Takèo)
First half of the VIth century (?)

Vishnu is shown here with eight arms and some unusual attributes which apparently make him into a sort of supreme god. Smaller statues of Rāma and Balarāma, both manifestations of Vishnu, surrounded this monumental statue forming a kind of trinity. A late inscription and stylistic characteristics led Pierre Dupont to attribute this work to the reign of Rudravarman I (514 -545).[1]

These statues would thus be the earliest dated with some degree of precision and could correspond to the waning art of Funan for which, so far, we had no undisputed sculptures. However, the arguments developed in favor of this attribution do not seem entirely convincing, and an appreciable updating of the images of the Phnom Dà group displaying the same characteristics should probably be further considered.

The frontal and hieratical stance which confers true grandeur upon Vishnu contrasts with his companions' supple and very Indian hip movement. The undeniable plastic qualities of the body notwithstanding, it denotes a greater quest for stately bearing than for anatomical truth, a truth not easily achieved when faced with the delicate problem of radiating four arms from a single shoulder.... The torso seems long and mostly modeled rather conventionally. The legs are short, but this too could merely be an ethnic characteristic comparable to the ones evidently mirrored in the wide oval of the face, the strongly arched nose and the narrow eyes. The beautifully shaped hands and feet should also be noted. While this work is one of the earliest known at this time, it denotes an art fulfilled and self-controlled where professional craftsmanship has long since replaced earlier hesitations.

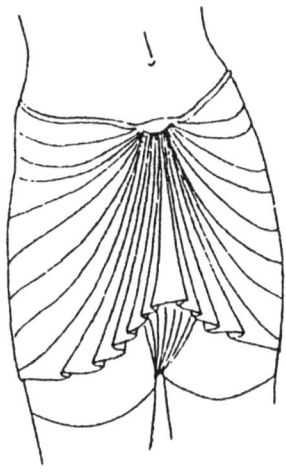

fig. A
Phnom Dà style "fan-shaped" male garment

---

[1]Pierre Dupont, "Les premières images brahmaniques d'Indochine," *Bulletin de La Société des Etudes indochinoises*, vol. XXVI, No. 2, pp. 131 ff., Saigon 1951.

The hair strands are shaped into long ringlets and spread about the nape in an arrangement inspired by India. The cylindrical mitre is also Indian, but the very simple loin-cloth drapery with soberly stylized "fan-shaped" pleats does not seem indebted to foreign models (fig. A).

After mentioning the sculptors' masterful execution, we must also call attention to their relative independence from Indian clichés. This independence indeed became one of the more salient traits of Khmer sculpture, and gave it its originality.

Carved in the round, the arms and the attributes would have been too fragile, so the artist turned to a device that remained in use until the early IXth century: a supporting arch that joins the units together, and insures overall solidity. This supporting arch, here in the shape of a horseshoe, or limited to the upper limbs as for the statue in Figure IV, is characteristic of almost all early Khmer sculpture. The use of this arch seems motivated by various considerations: recollection of images from India often treated in high relief, the need to support multiple arms and attributes, and a lack of confidence in the strength of the material used, be it schist or sandstone. In the case of schist, the chosen material of the early sculptors and lapicides, the caution is amply justified by the unfortunate tendency of the stone to cleave.

Note that no known feminine statue can be attributed to the Phnom Dà style. (Ed.)

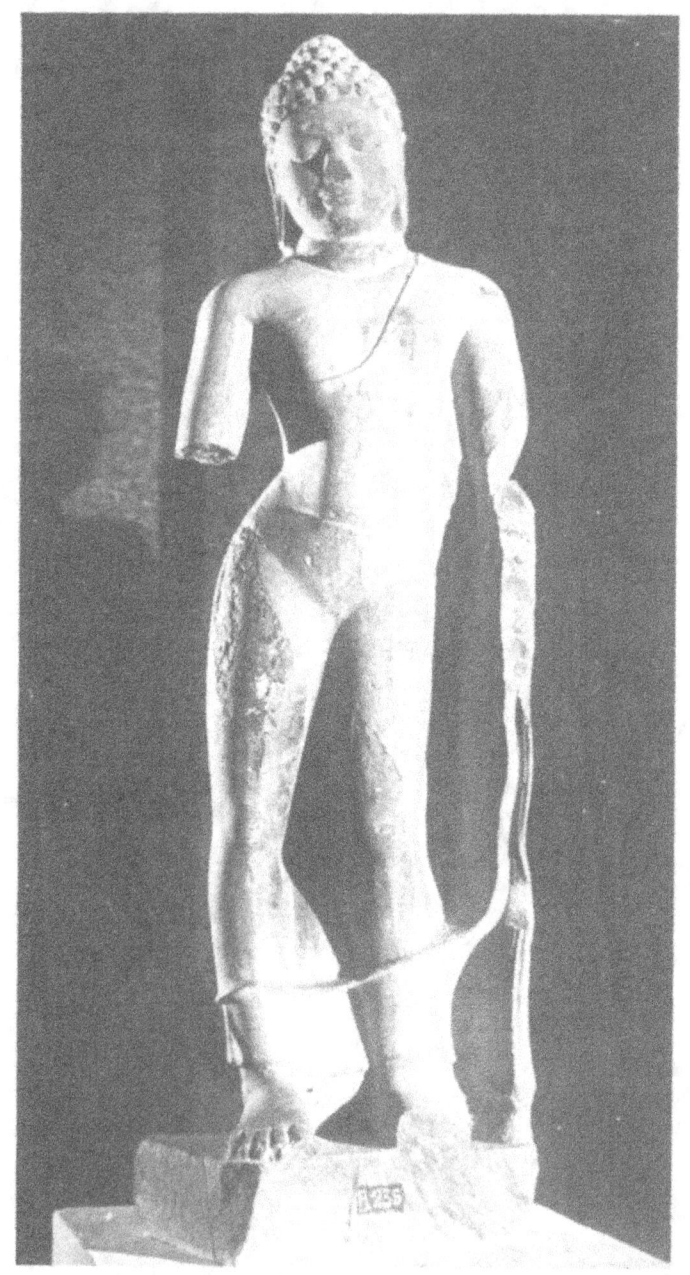

FIGURE II

FIGURE II

Standing Buddha (B-10, 14)

Sandstone (H. 1 m. 25—49 3/16"), Vat Romlok (Prei Krabas, Takèo)
VIth–VIIth centuries

This statue belongs to a group which can be considered as representative of the earliest Khmer Buddhist art, a group that shows more or less clear connections with India's Gupta and post-Gupta art,[1] but which also presents a number of original features. In Khmer art, the absence of the *ūrnā* in particular (a small tuft of hair between the eyebrows), is constant to this day.

The Buddha shown here holds a rather separate place in the development of the art. Most likely, he was shown making the gesture of charity; his hair done up in curls and the *ushnīsha* or cranial protuberance, all conform to the Indian tradition, but the drapery of the monastic garment and this image's posture distance him from that tradition. Philippe Stern felt that, in a way, these Buddhist images should be placed outside pre-Angkorian art[2] since they also differ almost as much from their contemporary Khmer types.

Clinging to the body like wet cloth, the monastic gown leaves the right shoulder bare, and falls naturally in the back with almost no indication of pleating. In India, statues that have one shoulder bare wear a concentrically pleated garment, and when smooth drapery becomes the norm it then covers both shoulders. And so, at the present time, it would seem that in the arts of India, outside of the great centers of Nālandā, whose art spans many centuries, and of Sri Lanka, the Vat Romlok Buddha has no clearly corresponding images.

The strongly *hanchée* (sway-hip) posture brings more to mind the one favored in the Mediterranean Basin than the Indian *tribhaṅga*, the triple flexion where the shoulder line and the hip line follow nearly parallel directions. The *hanchement* shown here, even though it is somewhat awkward, owes nothing to India and seems to be a recollection of a Western pose. The work is more that of a skillful artisan than of an expert. Many awkward features, such as the treatment of the eyes, tend to prove this. We are somewhat tempted to believe this work was a short-lived and probably unsuccessful attempt to adapt a posture that came from the West by way of Funan. The site of the find, made thanks to George Groslier, is located near the network of canals that connected present-day Angkor Borei to the sea coast of Funan. Moreover, excavations at Oc-èo have revealed that Roman objects, or objects having Hellenistic affinities, had entered Funan by sea. We do not believe that the model for this sculpture was a statue, nor that its date of execution was necessarily very early. The gaucheries we have pointed out seem to indicate that this work was inspired by a seal like the ones found at Oc-èo or the reverse side of a medal, and over-enlarged. Roman coins often show Olympian gods in the attitude depicted here, with a similar indication of volumes. Whatever merits this hypothesis may hold, the relative independence of Khmer sculptors from

---

[1]The Indian Gupta dynasty lasted from 320 to 510 A.D., but post-Gupta art may be extended past the VIIth century. (Ed.)

[2]Philippe Stern, "Esquisse d'une évolution de la statuaire," *Catalogue des Collections indochinoises du Musée Guimet* (Paris 1934).

Indian models appears very early in Buddhist and Brahmanic statuary as well, and cannot be stressed enough.

Nota. Recent discoveries[1] now lead us to think that we are probably looking at a statue of the Buddha of the Past Dīpankara whose images, ruled by a specific iconography, are encountered from the Malay Peninsula to the north of Borneo. But the Buddha found at Vat Romlok displays a number of outstanding characteristics that would tend to place him at the beginning of the series.

---

[1]J.Boisselier, "Le Buddha de Tuôl Tà Hoy et l'art bouddhique du Sud-Est asiatique" *Annales de l'Université Royale des Beaux-Arts*, Phnom Penh, année 1967, pp. 121 ff.

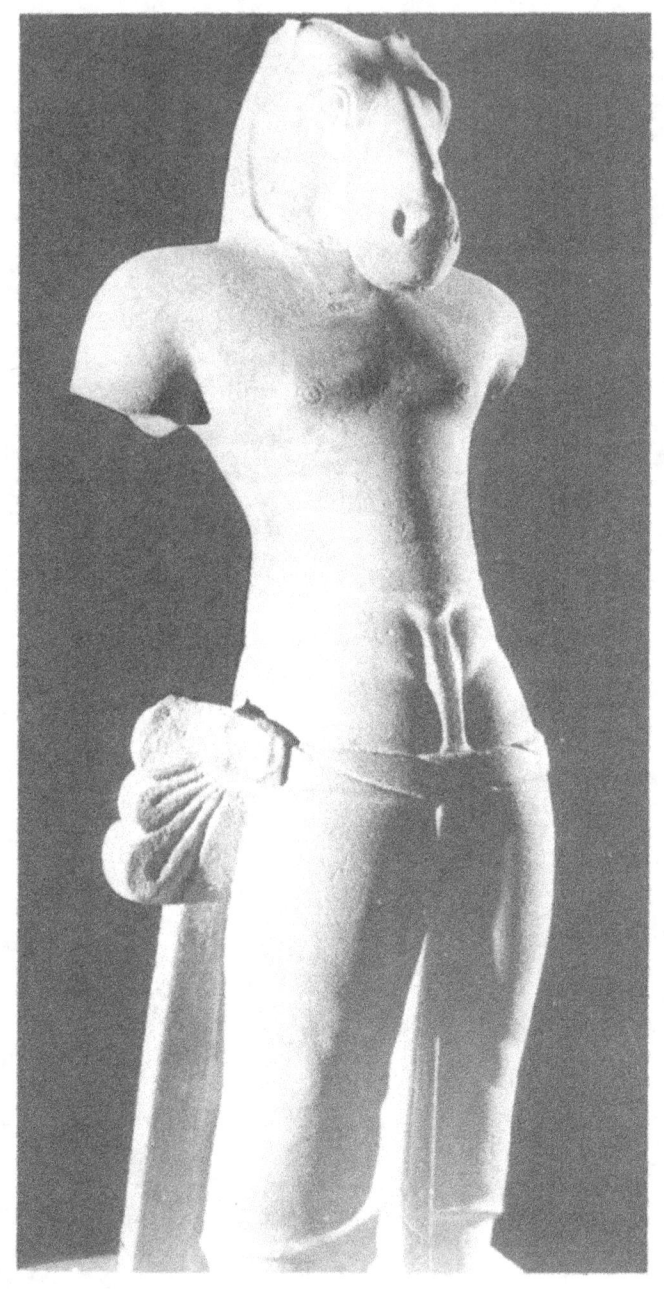

FIGURE III

FIGURE III

Vājimukha (B-31, 2)

Sandstone (H. 1 m. 35—53 5/16") found near the Kuk Trap village (Kandal)
Approximately VIIth century

Although the absence of the attributes prevents us from positively identifying this statue, it seems preferable to call it Vājimukha (face of horse), rather than Kalkin or Kalkyavatāra as is often done. And it so happens that Vājimukha was mentioned in XIth century Khmer epigraphy. It is one of the names for Hayagrīva, a minor *avatāra* of Vishnu struggling against Madhu and Kaitabha, the demons who stole the *Veda*. This episode was illustrated in the Xth century lintels of Prasat Thom at Koh Ker, and of Banteay Srei. But Kalkin, the 10th major *avatāra* and still not manifested, does not seem to appear either in Khmer epigraphy or art. As evidenced by the iconography of India, it would also seem that he is more likely to be depicted as a riding knight than as a hippocephalic divinity.

In contrast with the preceding statues, this astonishingly successful œuvre of the old Khmer artists reveals India's influences in the posture, the famous *tribhaṅga*, and in the costume, while its execution shows strong originality.

The sculptor managed to achieve the rare feat of bringing logic into the union of a human body with the head of a horse. He endowed it with a vitality that even Egyptian artists were unable to give their own similar works. Although Egyptians were the uncontested masters of animal art, their work remained hieratical.

Both the head of the horse and the human body are depicted here with surprising naturalism that does not exclude the simplification of volumes. The intricate problem of joining together two forms as dissimilar in their morphology as in their scale was resolved with great ingenuity: the artist invented a neck-line for the hybrid divinity. A real neck-line, be it equine or human, would point to the artificial nature of the composition. The one the artist selected, out of pure imagination and made to order, seems acceptable. Paradoxically larger than the head, the neck-line joins the shoulders with ease, and meets the lower jaw with the help of concave surfaces that restore the idea of volumes through a play of shadows, a method honored anew by XXth century decorators.

Faced with similar problems, later works did not attain the same technical achievement or naturalness.

With its long drapery, front panel, twisted belt, and large puffed bow on the hip, the costume was seen in contemporaneous India, but here the artist already interpreted it in a more liberal fashion. Oddly enough, we find that an image which seems to be one of the most closely related to India through its posture and the drapery of its garment, is also one, in our present state of knowledge, whose subject matter seems to have been the least used by Indian artists, especially at such an early date.

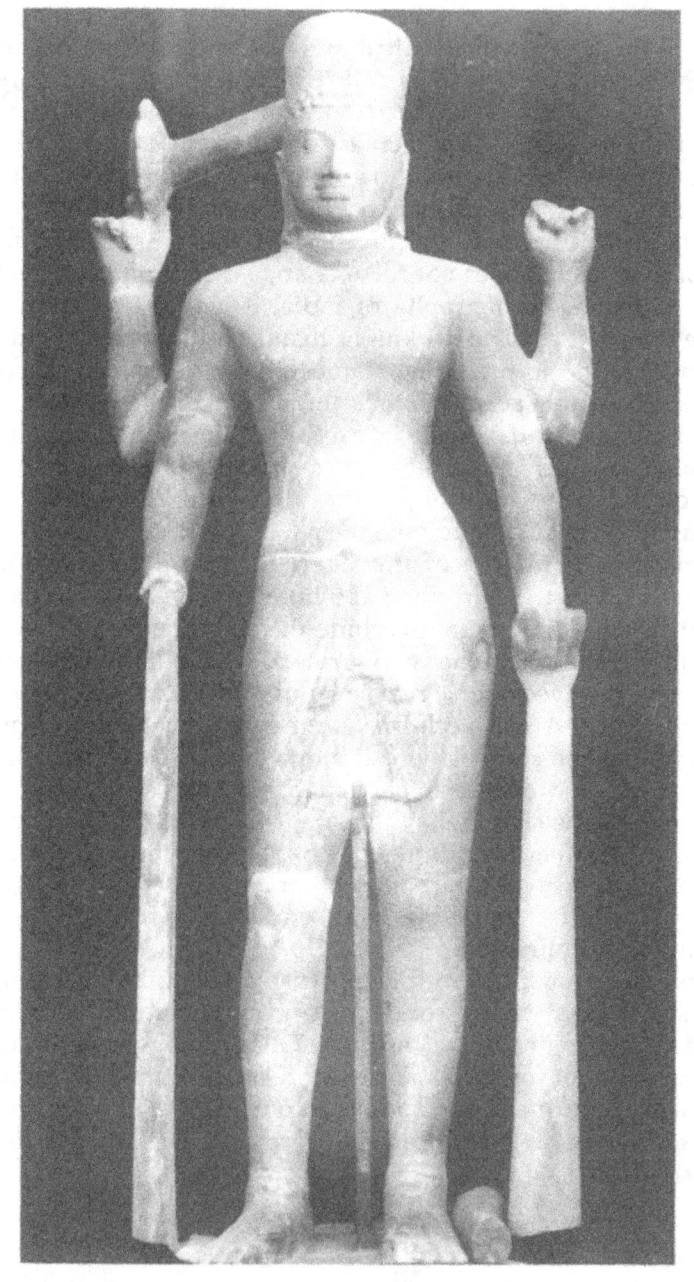

FIGURE IV

FIGURE IV

Vishnu (B-30, 15)

Sandstone (H. 1 m. 85—72 27/32"), found at Tûol Dai Buon
(Pearang, Prei Vèng)
VIIth century

In this statue Vishnu appears in the aspect in which he is most frequently shown: with four arms, holding the *cakra* (a disc-like weapon, and here his only surviving attribute), the conch, the mace, and a ball, which in Khmer art represents the Earth and replaces the lotus bud of Indian iconography. Like all images of Vishnu made before the mid-IXth century, he wears the cylindrical mitre we have previously mentioned for the Phnom Dà statue (Figure I). A royal symbol, this mitre, progressively covering more hair and enclosing more of the head, was eventually replaced by a diadem associated with a *mukuta*, a kind of head covering which, after undergoing many changes, has survived until now. But here the mitre, and the long ringlets are still very close to what they were at Phnom Dà.

Here the forms are full, and perhaps a little on the heavy side, but the statue shows some fine qualities. The modeling of the torso is executed with great restraint; the face is smiling and gentle, but it is quite different from what it became at the end of the XIIth century, tinged with a mysticism that does not appear here.

The somewhat awkward *hanchement*, marks one of the moments when Khmer art tried to free itself from a convention received from Indian models, but one ill-suited to its aesthetic ideal. Khmer art is less lascivious, and nearly always marked with grandeur and refined distinction.

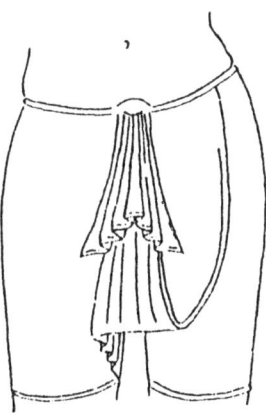

fig. B
Male garment related to that of Phnom Dà style "B"

The statue once had a supporting arch that joined only the head and the upper hands. Contrary to earlier beliefs, it seems that Khmer art simultaneously used the continuous horseshoe arch and a smaller arch limited to the upper limbs. The first one, the continuous horseshoe arch, was justified by the multiplicity of arms or by the fragility of the attributes. The second one, limited to the upper limbs, sufficed when, in images of Vishnu for example, one of the lower hands rested on the mace and the other on the puffed bow inspired by the Indian costume, and soon replaced by an actual support. To some extent, these different techniques probably resulted from work-shop traditions, but a practical concern dictated by the fragility of the attributes may also be a reason for it. This is why most images of Vishnu only have the smaller arch whereas images of Harihara keep the horseshoe arch. It was not until the semi-anarchy of the VIIIth century, when artists copied and often interpreted earlier models with uneven success, that they made indiscriminate use of the horseshoe arch or of the smaller one.

In this statue the garment (fig. B), which is related to the Phnom Dà style "B"[1] shows the "anchor-shaped" drapery in front which, with continuous modifications, characterizes most Khmer male statuary of subsequent styles, and the still sketchy "pocket-fold" on the left hip that became very apparent in the Harihara from Prasat Andèt (Figure VI). (Ed.)

---

[1]Jean Boisselier, *Le Cambodge*, p. 238.

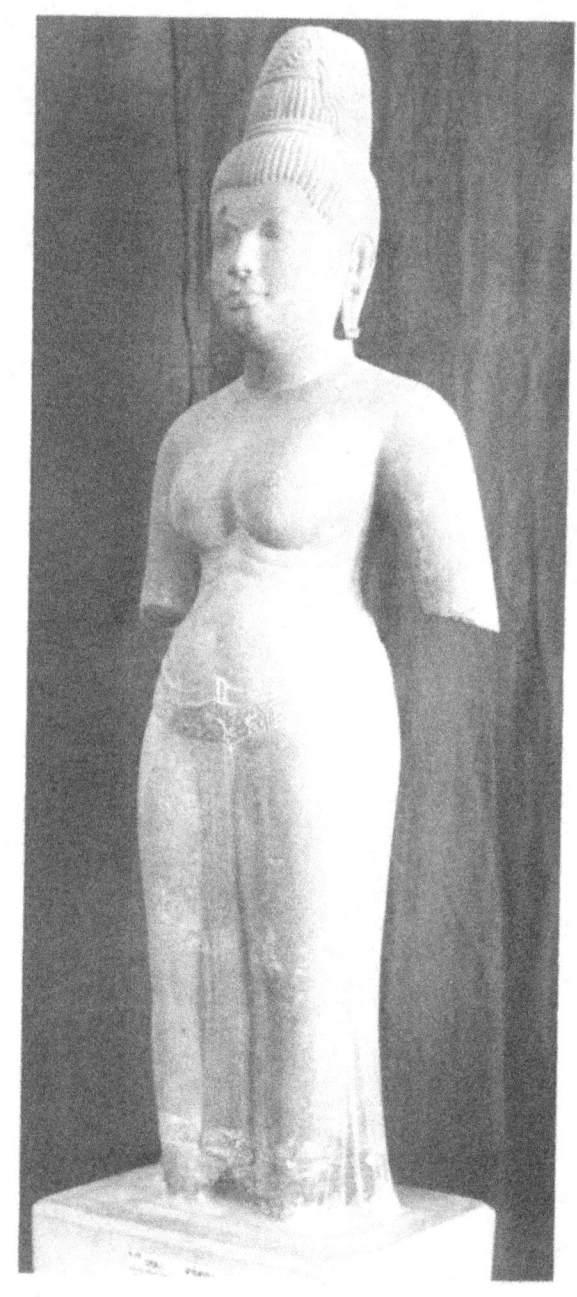

FIGURE V

FIGURE V

Feminine Divinity (B-71, 1)
Sandstone (H. 1 m. 27—50"), Koh Krieng (Kompong Cham)
VIIth century

This statue, possibly representing Lakshmī, Vishnu's *śakti*, or Devī, Śiva's *śakti*, cannot be positively identified for want of the attributes once held in the now missing hands.

It is the most beautiful feminine image which to our knowledge predates the end of the IXth century. While representations of feminine divinities are quite frequent during the earliest period, their artistic qualities are generally mediocre. Small in size, with an often awkward *hanchement*, and bulging eyes, they do not represent, as was long believed, the halting experiments of an art at its beginning. They do, on the contrary, seem to characterize the output of decadent ateliers of the VIIIth century awkwardly inspired by earlier models, very few of which have survived for us to see.

Some details of the hair-style, the adornment, and the drapery of the skirt, tend to suggest that the Koh Krieng divinity is a work of the 2nd half of the VIIth century, probably following very closely the reign of Īśānavarman I, the founder of Sambor Prei Kuk.

The high degree of perfection the sculptor attained was hardly ever encountered again, except a century or so later in the famous Harihara from Prasat Andèt (Figure VI). In this image, all recollection of *hanchement* has vanished. In spite of its total frontal stance, the work is fully alive and the modeling, expressed very soberly, shows remarkable observation. The body is that of a woman in the prime of life whose opulent forms are dictated by Indian tradition but are stripped of India's overflowing sensuality.

These forms, so directly inspired by reality, remained the feminine canon *par excellence* until just about the end of the XIIth century; but they underwent a progressive stylization that reached its climax in the early Xth century.

With its well-delineated oval, aquiline nose, full and fleshed lips, the face is quite majestic. As usual, the ear lobes are greatly distended with their lower part perforated to accommodate mobile pendants.

The hair is dressed in a complicated high chignon reminiscent of the ascetics' coiffure adopted for certain representations of Śiva. But it should be noted that it is Lakshmī who seems to show a preference for this chignon while Śiva's *śakti* usually wears Vishnu's mitre, and what is more, she also has his attributes.

The skirt clings to the body it closely molds. It has only one set of center folds, and a few very plain lateral folds. The skirt reveals the abdomen, and is held in place by a belt whose finely engraved buckle shows a decoration of purely Indian inspiration (fig. C). Most feminine statues which we believe should be attributed to the VIIIth century have a skirt that no longer bares the abdomen. It is decorated with a sketchy pleating shown by simple engraved lines and ornamented with a rounded "pocket" overhanging the belt (fig. D). That particular drapery inspired the Banteay Srei sculptors in the 2nd half of the Xth century.[1]

---

[1]It can be seen on the Devatā in high relief (fig. E), but it should be noted that no free-standing feminine divinity is known in the Banteay Srei style. (Ed.)

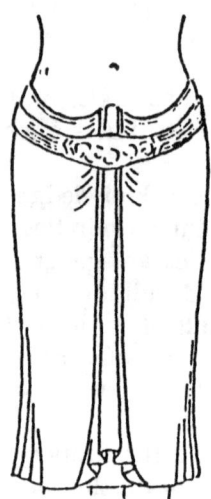

fig. C
Koh Krieng Feminine Divinity
Style of Sambor

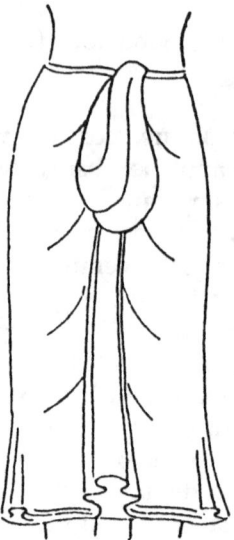

fig. D
Feminine Divinity
Kompong Spu'

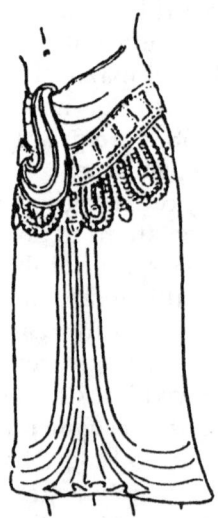

fig. E
Devatā
High relief *in situ*
Banteay Srei

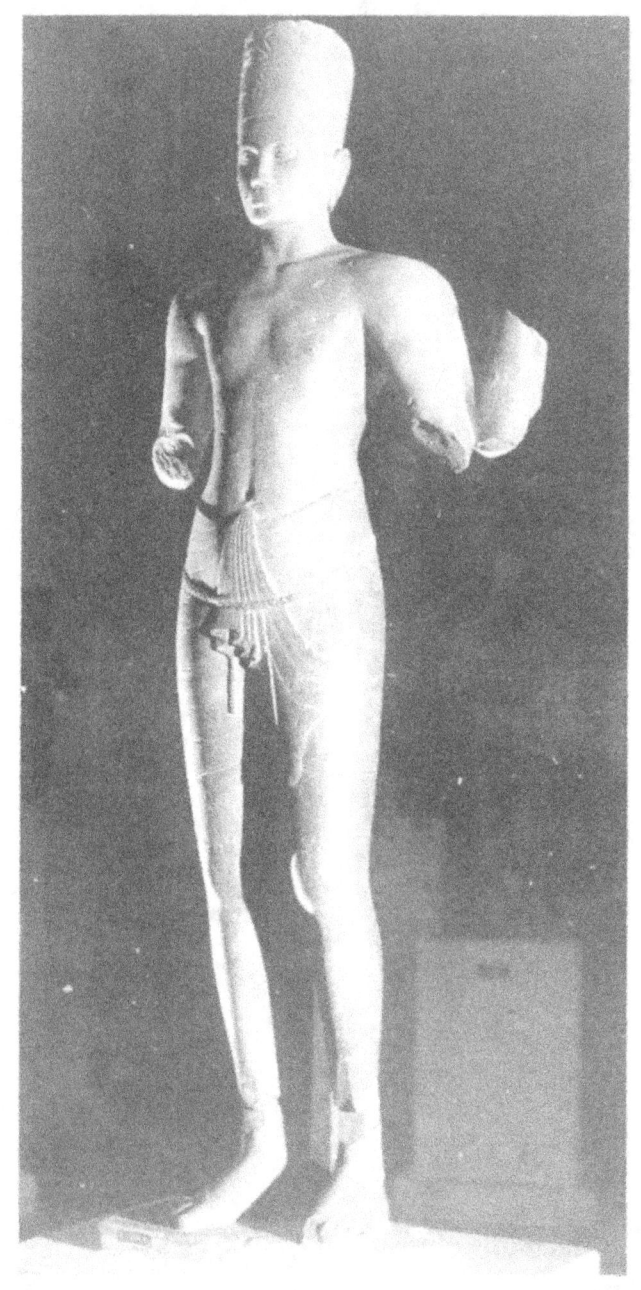

FIGURE VI

FIGURE VI

Harihara (B-45, 1)

Sandstone (H. 1 m. 94—76 3/8") Prasat Andèt
(Stu'ng, Kompong Thom)
End of VIIth–VIIIth century

Despite the loss of the attributes, Harihara can easily be identified, thanks to the composite nature of the headdress.

Harihara, the mixed divinity whose right side is made in the image of Śiva and left side in that of Vishnu, was very popular in Cambodia, especially in the earliest period. This duality explains the hybrid composition of the headdress made up on the right side of half a chignon inspired by the chignon of the ascetics, and of half of Vishnu's mitre on the left side. Moreover, the statue's forehead bears half of Śiva's third vertical eye. Earlier images had in their chignon the crescent moon which is no longer shown here. In fact, it seems that over the centuries the divinity's Śivaite characteristics increasingly faded out and gradually gave way to Vishnuite features.

This Harihara, perhaps the most famous statue in the Phnom Penh Museum, is the œuvre where the sculptors carried anatomical accuracy to the highest degree of perfection through precise and discreet modeling. It is the only work where the musculature in the back is shown. Just as in Figure V, and even more so, the blend of a somewhat hieratic feeling with naturalism results in a highly poised nobleness. The Museum's presentation unfortunately shows the work with an excessive elongation of the legs due only to a faulty restoration. Through an error of appraisal, the statue was reassembled with a Western hip movement in mind, whereas its very slight *hanchement* was only a recollection of the Indian *tribhaṅga*. The restorer was thus misled to raise the ankles with an unnecessary addition of cement, and the statue's proportions should be a little stockier, but also more accurate.

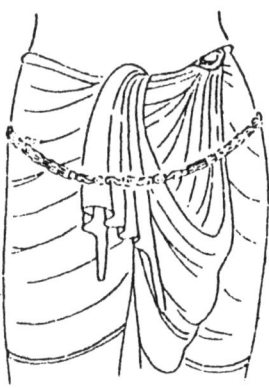

fig. F
Harihara from Prasat Andèt

The treatment of the head shows the same quest for vitality and grandeur as in the previously described feminine divinity. But the ethnic type is altogether different. The nose is absolutely straight, the strong chin and the well modeled eyes give it somewhat of a hard expression which is exceptional in Khmer art. It should be noted that the upper lip is edged by a thin moustache, probably making one of its first appearances here, but which remained the rule until approximately the end of the Xth century.

Compared to the earliest forms, the costume has evolved considerably (fig. F). Given a few more minor changes it will grow into a style that Khmer statuary followed almost consistently. The "pocket-fold" we first noticed in Figure IV is still free here. Later on it was raised to the belt and lay against the thigh, and a cloth belt, whether or not combined with an "anchor-shaped" front drapery, replaced the metal belt. This one is made of a fine chainlet whose clasp is adorned with beautiful Indian-like scrolls. It is not without certain analogies, previously mentioned by George Groslier,[1] to the chain fragment found at Kbal Romeas, and presented to the Museum by S.M. Sisowath in 1916. Note that the lower part of the headgear is enhanced by a narrow decorated headband which may be seen as a first step towards the diadem style which will be so much in vogue in later years.

Despite its litheness and masterly execution, the statue was made with a supporting arch in the shape of a horseshoe still visible in the back of the arms. Its only justification is the fragility of the trident, a Śivaite attribute.

---

[1] George Groslier, "Les Collections khmères du Musée Albert-Sarraut," p. 122, Pl. XLVIII, 1 (*Ars Asiatica,* vol. XVI, Paris, 1931).

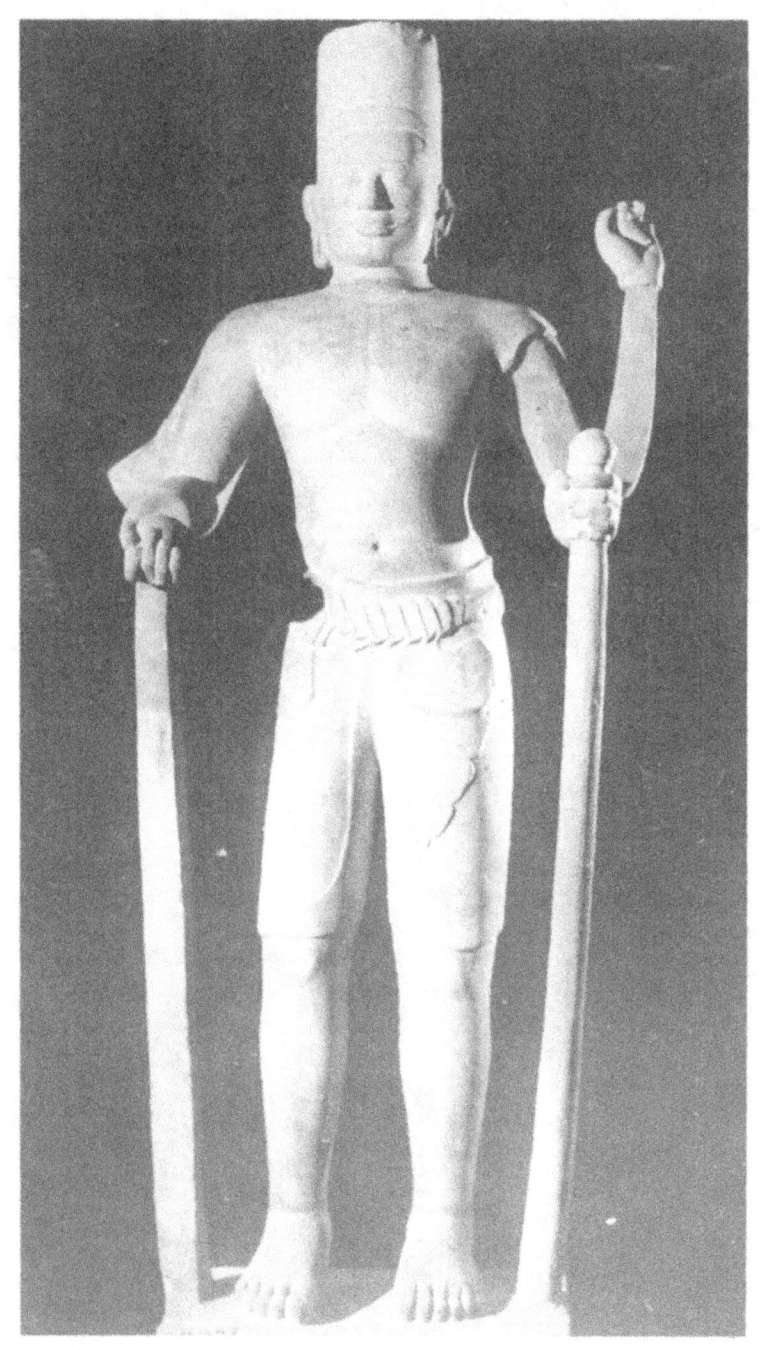

FIGURE VII

FIGURE VII

Vishnu (B-30, 21)

Sandstone (H. 1 m. 73—68 1/8") Prasat Thmà Dap (Phnom Kulên)
First half of the IXth century

This was the first statue of the Kulên style that the Phnom Penh Museum acquired. The *Kulên style*, defined in 1936 thanks to Ph. Stern's work, most likely corresponds to the founding of Mahendraparvata during the reign of Jayavarman II on Phnom Kulên. Historically, it marks the birth of the Angkorian monarchy by the initiation of the *Devarāja cult*. From an artistic standpoint, it indicates the transition between the old forms and the ones that asserted themselves during some four centuries to come.

New sculptural schemes established themselves during the reign of Jayavarman II; the old traditions faded away and the renewal of themes and a quest for new forms characterized both statuary and decor.

The Prasat Thmà Dap was one of the last shrines erected on Phnom Kulên, and this Vishnu is an excellent example of the spirit of the style. While it is already quite close to what the statuary became in the next few decades it nevertheless continues the previous period. The mitre, in particular, appears here for the last time.

The body has lost its slenderness and is headed for a kind of "well fed" ideal that was to rule male statuary for the next hundred or so years. The torso shows the handsome qualities of discreet modeling observed in previous centuries. The old *hanchement* seems to have been retained by sheer force of habit, but it is awkward and one feels that it is on the verge of being given up. The face is almost like the one the sculptors adopted in the *Prah Kô style* less than a century later. A face which is wider than before, a little heavy, and marked by an air of self-sufficiency; it has an up-turned moustache, prominent, unbroken orbital ridges, and it is very far from the aesthetic ideal that had prevailed until then. While the mitre is still retained, its shape has evolved considerably and it will never be shown again. Moreover, in the same Thmà Dap monument appeared the first diadems, an element of the royal coiffure with which Vishnu, the universal monarch *par excellence*, was immediately endowed.

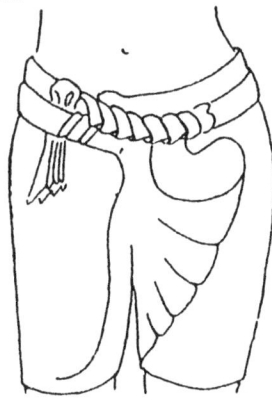

fig. G
Vishnu from Prasat Thmà Dap (Phnom Kulên)

The costume also has a new look (fig. G). It is directly derived from that of the Prasat Andèt Harihara (Figure VI), but the "pocket-fold" has now reached its ultimate location, and the cloth belt makes its first appearance. While the *sampot* is still smooth, the pleating that was to acquire a growing importance is beginning to take shape.

The supporting arch, kept for only one Kulên statue and it was an earlier one, is done away with; the device is definitely abandoned.

By far, not all works of the *Kulên style* echo a single type; some are closer descendants of the past, and others, as this one does, more closely herald the future. But each has some characteristic it can call its own, which is an essential feature in a period of renewal.

We might add that the statue's equilibrium, far poorer than in most pieces of the style, is further impaired by damages that led to an unflattering restoration which is of little help in bringing out the very real plastic qualities of the work.

It is noteworthy that at the present time there are no known feminine statues of the *Kulên style*. (Ed.)

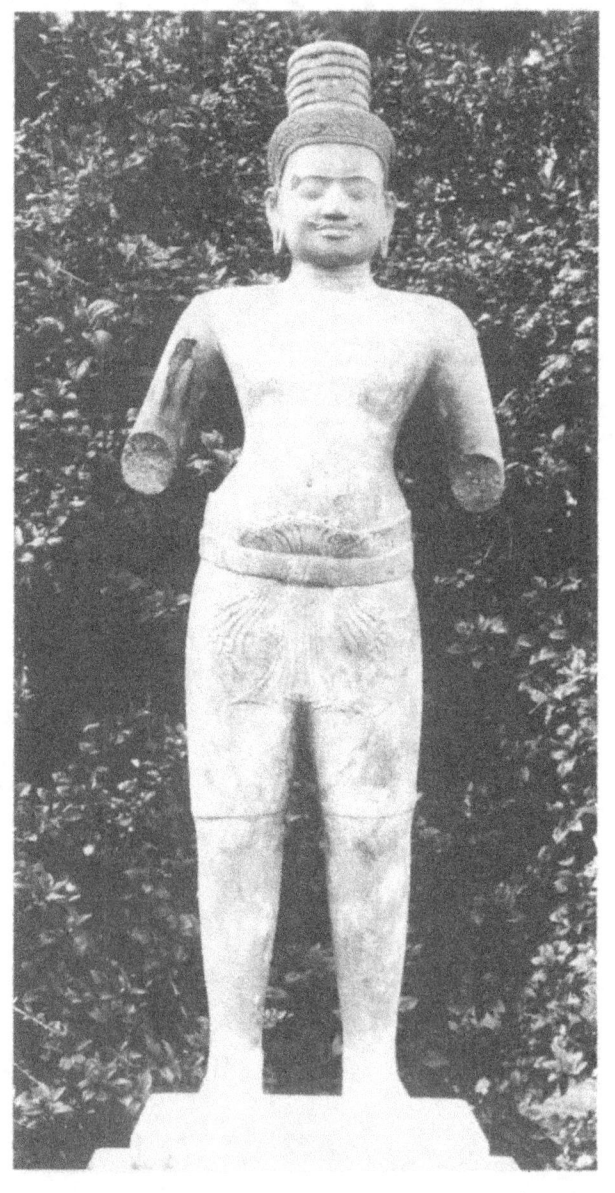

FIGURE VIII

FIGURE VIII

Śiva (B-40, 5)

Sandstone (H. 1 m. 87—73 5/8"), Bàkong (Rolûoh)
Third quarter of IXth century

This image is remarkably characteristic of the statuary of the *Prah Kô style*. It corresponds to the capital of Indravarman and immediately precedes the founding of the first Angkor. Earlier trends of the Kulên style were carried into the Prah Kô style where they burst forth, underscoring a new plastic orientation that seems to have completely broken off with traditions that predate the middle of the IXth century. Some of the innovations perpetuated themselves until the end of the Angkor period.

Śiva is represented here in human form. Following a convention peculiar to Khmer art, he wears the *jatāmukuta* or crown of hair, the chignon of the ascetics made up of small tiered loops. This convention was established at the end of the Kulên style, but it already had its roots in the VIIIth century. This chignon bears the crescent moon and the divinity's forehead has a simply engraved third vertical eye.

Regardless of what has been said about it, the body still shows, but for the last time, the *hanchement* we noticed in most of the earlier works. The modeling is headed for the conventional forms of the first half of the Xth century, but as usual it is only suggested. The preference for a hieratical stance, plus a certain architectural feeling, favor stockier forms that seek a stately grandeur shown by the marked stoutness of the individual, and the more austere and idealized expression of the face. We have previously noted that this was all latent in the Kulên style whose code has now established itself, conforming to a new aesthetic. The fashionable slight portliness may not be without ties to Javanese art whose influence was somewhat felt in the decorative art of the period. This observation could probably be stretched to the particular appearance of the chignon. But the facial expression and the composition of the finely engraved diadem are, in any case, very Khmer. We also note that the narrow diadem is peculiar to the style. The face is treated in the same spirit as at Thmà Dap (Figure VII), and indicates only a new advance towards stylization: the moustache is more pronounced, the short beard is rendered in a very conventional way, the orbital ridges are prominent, unbroken, and almost sharp, the eyes are bulging.

The costume is also in the Kulên tradition where some statues show, as this one does, the front "anchor-shaped" drapery and the "pocket-fold," and the same wide belt (fig. H). Here still

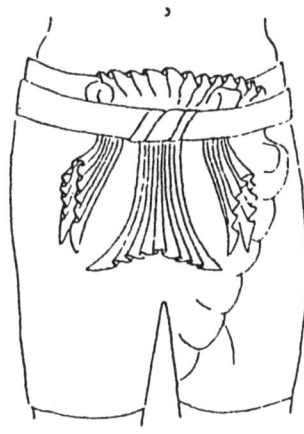

fig. H
Śiva from Bàkong (Rolûoh)
Prah Kô style

limited and quite naturalistic, the pleating begins to acquire a growing importance. In the next style it will take over the entire garment and become even more stylized.[1]

Images of Śiva did not become frequent until the Prah Kô style. Up to that time they were exceptional, and it seems that originally the divinity was almost entirely represented in the phallic and symbolic aspect of the *liṅga*.

---

[1]It should be noted that in this next style, the Bàkheng style (after 893–ca. 927), a new stylization of the ears also occurred. The ear conch became tri-lobed (cf. Jean Boisselier, *La Statuaire khmère et son évolution*, page 172), i.e., it was made up of three "scrolls"; this stylization continued, with minor modifications, all through the Bàyon Style. But in the Banteay Srei style there are only two "scrolls," and in the Angkor Vat style, there are either three, or sometimes only two "scrolls." (Ed.)

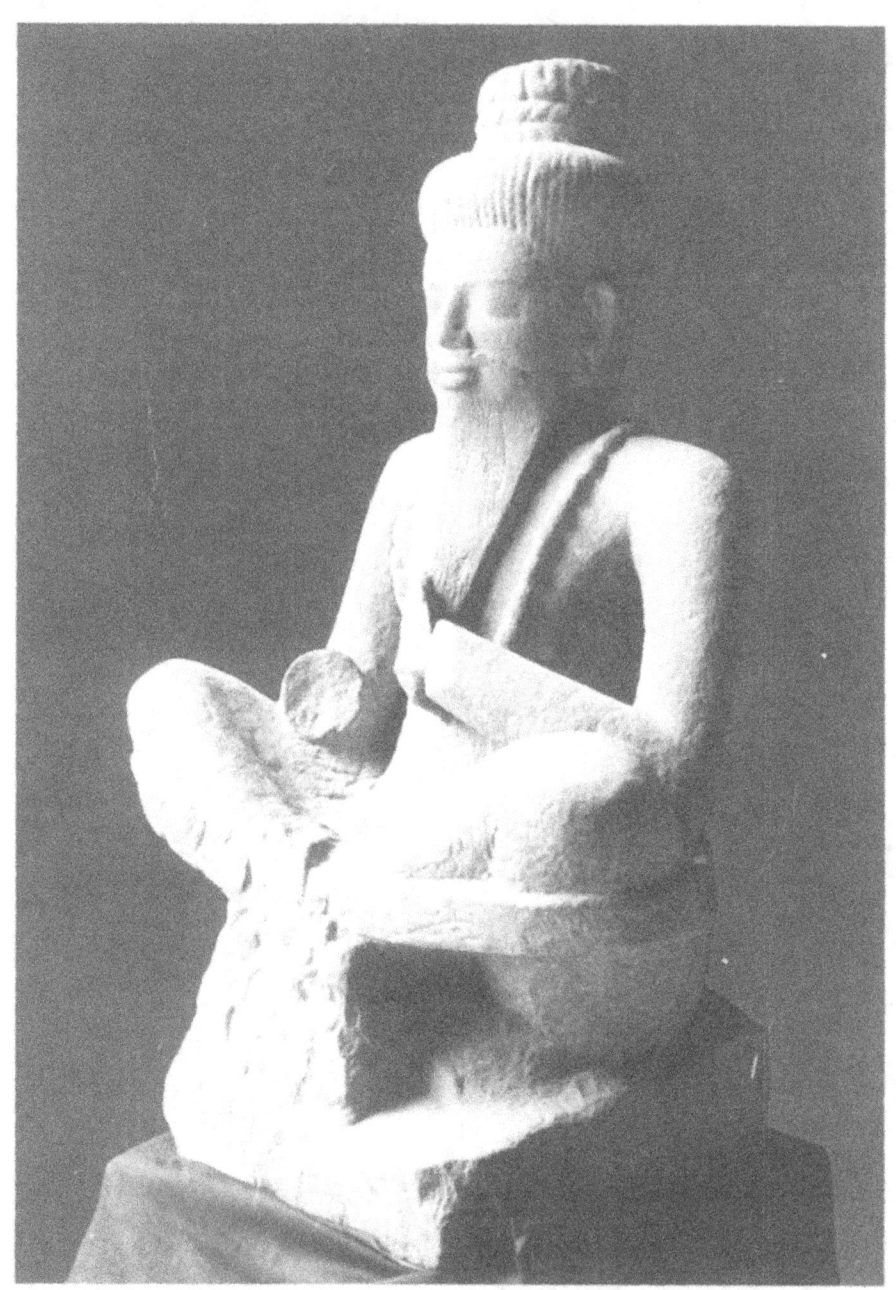

FIGURE IX

FIGURE IX

Ascetic at Prayer (B-62, 4)

Sandstone (H. 0 m. 50—19 11/16") Prah Kô (Rolûoh)
Third quarter of IXth century

This sculpture in the round came from one of the superstructures of Prah Kô where it served as an antefix. Antefix figures can be seen in all Khmer monuments built with lasting materials; but while this one was treated as a free-standing piece, in most cases the figure was shown against a background, and appeared in high relief. Antefix figures vary greatly: they depict Indra armed with his thunderbolt, guardians holding their trident, spear, or mace; *apsaras;* divinities mounted on their *vāhana;* and most of all, ascetics at prayer, as this one is, or promoted to the role of guardians.... All these figures who adorn the roofing levels tend to make the sanctuary into an image, visible from afar, of the mountain abode of the gods. We see this represented on a pediment of Banteay Srei in the guise of a pyramid where each tier is occupied by various beings. Since the inner chamber of the shrine was only accessible to the officiants, it was normal that its outside view should be magnified for the benefit of all those who did not have the privilege of entering it.

The ascetic represented here is at prayer, with joined hands, with knees held together with a strap, as in India, which helps him to maintain the most propitious attitude.

The long beard, and the hair gathered up in a high chignon are characteristic of the ascetics; note the similarity between this headdress and that of Śiva in Figure VIII.

We must also mention that the sacred (Brahmanic) thread is exceptional in Cambodia, and that a necklace made up of large beads seems to replace it in this image.

While the face indicates a trend towards the simplification of volumes, it also reflects extreme gentleness and serenity, and an almost ecstatic expression.

In this work, meant only to be seen from a distance and included in an architectural decor, there is a deeply religious feeling that could be foreshadowing by three centuries the mysticism of the Bàyon. Whereas the ideal for these divinities consisted of rather impersonal grandeur, some of these heads of ascetics attained a deep vital strength that makes them into unquestionable masterpieces. Similar examples can be found at Thmà Dap in the Kulên style.

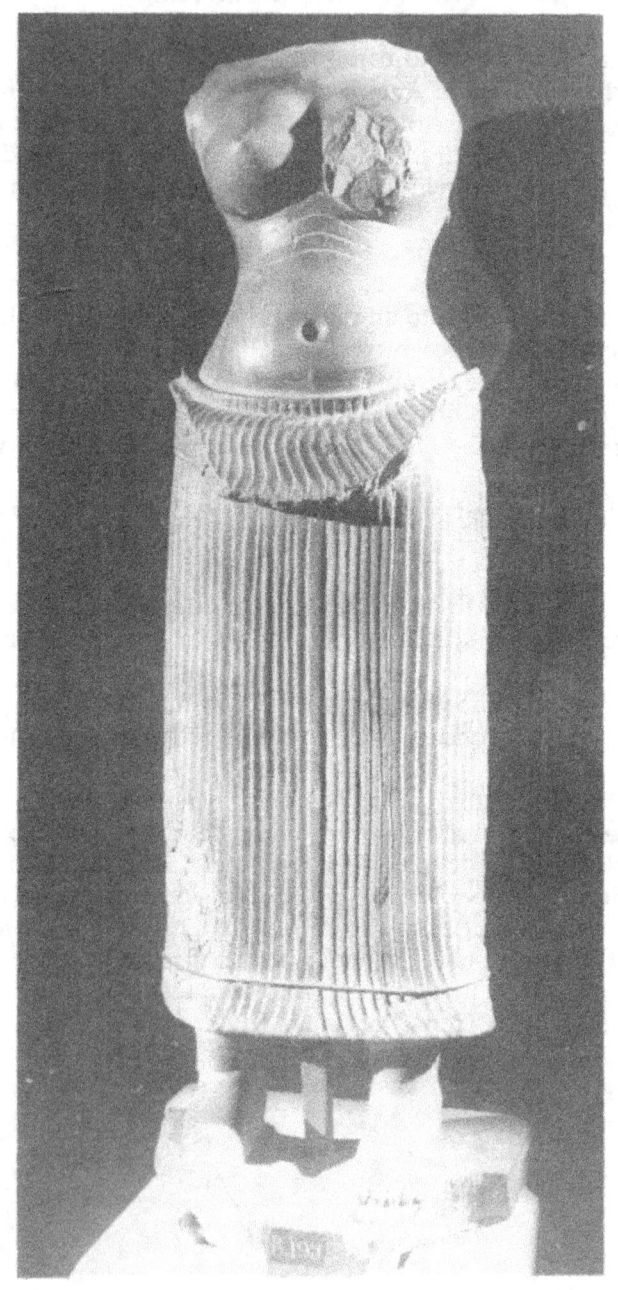

FIGURE X

FIGURE X

Body of Feminine Divinity (B-422, 1)
Sandstone (H. 1 m. 08—42 17/32")
Prasat Neang Khmau, North shrine (Bàti, Takèo)[1]
First half of Xth century

It is this divinity, unfortunately mutilated, who gave her name to the monument that sheltered her: the Shrine of the Black Lady. The "Black Lady" is none other than Kālī, the destructive aspect of Śiva's *śakti*. But this appellation recalls less her identity—very hypothetical for that matter, since the monument's only surviving frescoes are Vishnuite—than the color of the stone out of which she is carved: dark, almost greenish blue, and exceptionally beautiful.

Despite its condition when it came to us, the œuvre thoroughly conveys the stylistic ideal of hieratical posture that ruled the statuary of the *Bàkheng style* which corresponds to Yaśovarman's founding of the first Angkor. While the work is slightly later than his reign (the inscription of the shrine dates it to 928 A.D.), it shows all the characteristics of the style: its complete frontality and its forms are stylized to the utmost with deference to the early canons which dictated wide hips and full breasts.[2] The "beauty folds" of the breasts are retained, but they are translated by parallel incisions which no longer reflect observation of the living model.

The garment has greatly evolved. The skirt is enhanced with regular, mechanical, and unrealistic pleats which are retained, in sculpture in the round, up to the last years of the XIIth century. But the drapery, conversely, underwent constant modifications. The contour of the skirt's upper part was greatly altered, and yet an almost similar turned-down edge reappeared in the XIIth century style of Angkor Vat.

The highly architectural conception of the work is also seen in the male images of this style. The ideal of grandeur and power has obliterated all concern for anatomical truth, but its success was short-lived and barely survived the middle of the century when the Banteay Srei reaction occurred, one which had a completely opposite spirit.

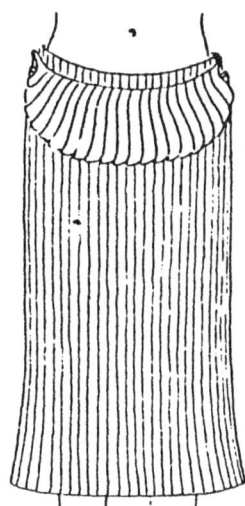

fig. I
Garment of Koh Ker Feminine Divinity
in situ, Prasat Chrap (Koh Ker)

---

[1]Approximately 35 kilometers south of Phnom Penh. (Ed.)

[2]Although the date of this sculpture follows by a few years the establishment of the short-lived capital at Koh Ker (921–944) situated 85 kilometers north-east of Angkor, its findspot, located some 280 kilometers from Koh Ker, and the absence of the head and of the head-dress which could provide valuable stylistic information, do not allow us to attribute this image to the Koh Ker style (fig. I). (Ed.)

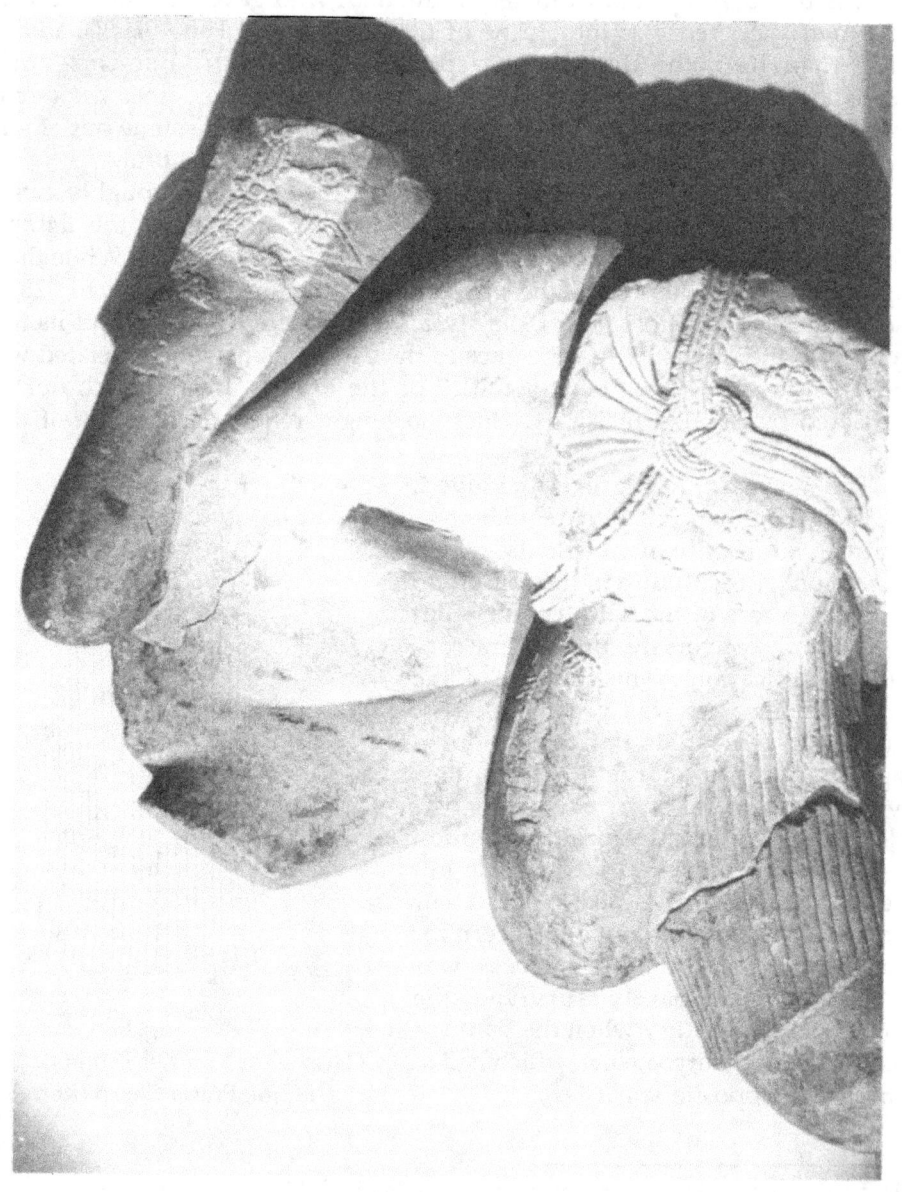

FIGURE XI

FIGURE XI

Group of Wrestlers (B-702, 56)
Sandstone (H. 0 m. 80—31 1/2") Prasat Thom (Koh Ker)
Second quarter of Xth century

The identity of these wrestlers is impossible to ascertain. Judging by the costumes, the scene is probably a fight between a *deva* wearing a pleated costume and an *asura* whose apparel is richly embellished with pendants. Tales of fights between benevolent and demonical beings abound throughout many long epic narratives, and given the group's present state of preservation one cannot venture the slightest hypothesis as to the episode that may be illustrated here.

The dynamic force of such a group is unexpected in Khmer statuary whose preference for hieratical forms we have so often emphasized. Some have even attempted to make the art of Koh Ker the high point of this trend. But in fact, the style of Jayavarman IV's short-lived capital was highly innovative and also very complex because of the different trends that confronted each other there. In this style the statuary assumed the most varied aspects through its expressions and in the choice of themes. Hieratical stances and a feeling for architectural grandeur were confronted with an astonishing sense of motion. With the biggest statues and the largest monuments that Khmer talent ever dared, Koh Ker united all at once a strong liking for the colossal, and for action.

Nowhere else have sculptural groups enjoyed the same vogue as at Koh Ker where the statuary, static or in motion, bears witness to a creative originality that was not to be found in later times.

However, in this style, no other sculpture in the round can claim the successful result achieved by the museum group. The authenticity of the attitudes, the suppleness of the movements, and the simplification of the discreetly suggested volumes all make it an unparalleled work. As in a dance, the struggle is implied by gesture with no indication of effort. Muscular contractions would ill-suit supernatural beings, and Khmer art has never allowed itself to show passion in any form whatsoever, be it in divine or simply human beings. This is not due to artistic ignorance or to inability, contrary to what could easily be presumed. It is rather a convention similar to the ones that ruled so many Western arts: Egypt or classical Greece. Passion, for Khmer sculptors, seems incompatible with the dignity of a god or even of a human being. But this convention ceases to apply to monkeys for instance unless, of course, they happen to hold a very high rank. If we examine the bas-reliefs of Angkor Vat, made approximately two hundred years after our wrestlers, we see these monkeys, *Rāma's* allies, overflowing with passion, fighting, all muscles flexed with extraordinary exertion, crying from true sorrow, prancing about or laughing wholeheartedly with amazing vitality. It also seems that from the XIIth century on this vitality and realism continued to expand until the naturalistic outburst of the Bàyon period.

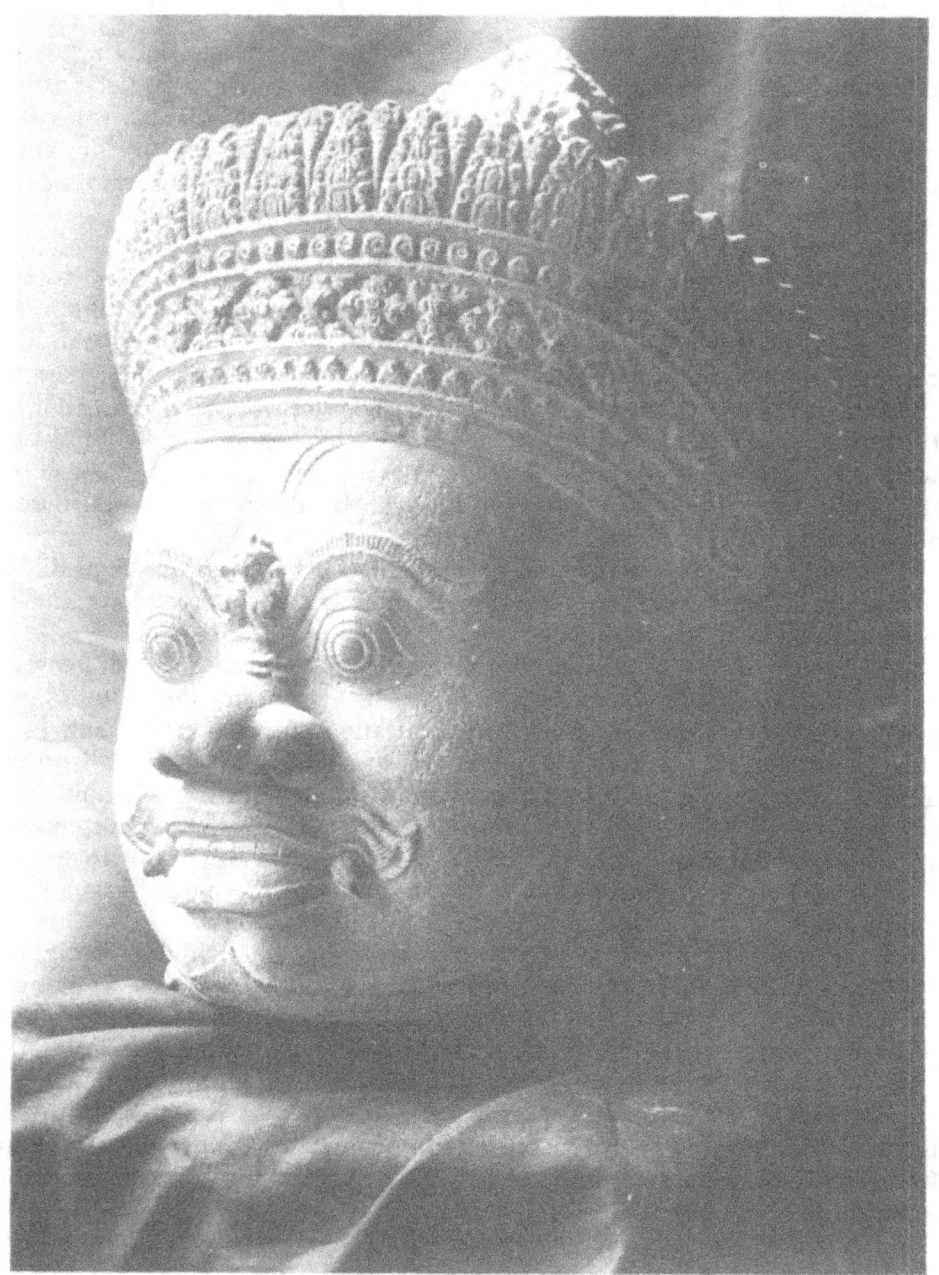

FIGURE XII

FIGURE XII

Fierce Looking Head (B-611, 5)

Pink sandstone (H. 0 m. 40—15 3/4") Prasat Thom (Koh Ker)
Second quarter of Xth century

This personage, in guise of some *yaksha*, would be one of the gate-keepers standing guard and bearing arms at the entrance of sanctuaries, or kneeling at prayer on pedestals flanking short flights of steps leading to a shrine. In Cambodia, this attitude seems to be limited to the 2nd and 3rd quarters of the Xth century.

Whatever his actual identity and attitude might be, this personage has been endowed by the sculptor with a terrifying mask that is in accordance with India's iconographic traditions. But such an expression reflects passion, and we have seen that Khmer art banished it as much as it did horror. Thus the artist tried to translate the emotion in a manner that would be more compatible with his artistic ideal.

The round and popping eyes, the wide nose with distended nostrils, the frowning forehead, the wrinkles, the lips revealing the teeth, the protruding fangs are all called for in the texts and make up the arsenal of convincing anger. The artist respected these principles, but he backed away from everything too naturalistic, and has treated his subject like a decorator. The pupils of the eyes are made of concentric circles; the nose springs out from a decorated palmette; the eyebrows, beard, and moustache are stylized to the utmost, and the adornment completes the overall impression. The rich diadem with rosettes above the ears, which are mostly intended for this type of individual, the *mukuta* adorned with a beautiful motif made of wide petals, and the large foliate branches that decorate the helmet over the nape, add the finishing touches that give the work a decorative meaning.

Contrary to the convention that was adopted for images of divinities, heavy pendants adorn these ears. Their shape is unexpected because this particular one is usually meant for benevolent characters; fierce beings preferably wear discs or heavy rings.

It seems that the differentiation between the two categories of gate-keepers, benevolent or fierce, became lesser with time. It was much more pronounced in the Prah Kô period when the fierce character wore a voluminous crop of hair that has vanished now. During the XIth century he became almost similar to his companion. We have to wait for the Angkor Vat period for the differences to appear again, and end in the clear-cut types of the Bàyon period.

The very fine craftsmanship of this head, enhanced by the exceptional quality of the sandstone, is particularly noteworthy. It does well in summarizing some of the more stable features of Khmer statuary: its decorative meaning, moderation in the expression, conceptual broadness, and minuteness of its execution.

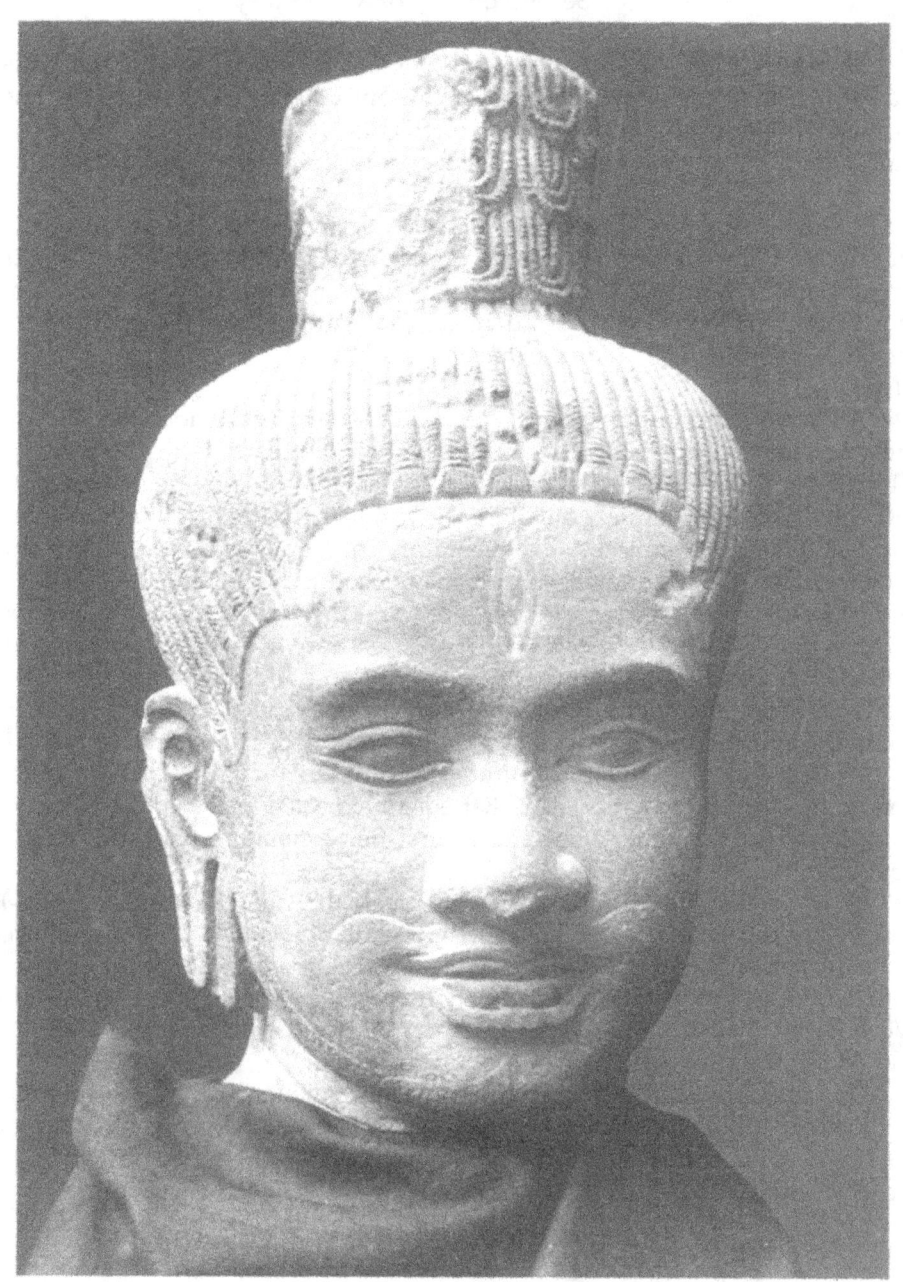

FIGURE XIII

FIGURE XIII

Head of Deva (B-601, 4)

Pink Sandstone (H. 0 m. 32—12 19/32") Banteay Srei (Siem Reap)
Third quarter of Xth century

One could easily take this delicate head for an image of Śiva because of the vertical eye on the forehead. It actually belongs to one of those personages with a human or an animal head, kneeling on pedestals flanking the steps of the Banteay Srei temple, as those of the Prasat Thom at Koh Ker. During the anastylosis work H. Marchal conducted at Banteay Srei between 1931 and 1936, most figures could be reassembled and returned to their original location. The body of this one was never identified with certainty.

The art of Banteay Srei can be characterized by two trends: the traditional one which in a way carries on the principles worked out during earlier styles; the other, innovative, is inspired by earlier models from the VIIth to the IXth centuries. The first trend is principally represented by statues of divinities, while the second one is more involved in everything decorative. A quest for beauty and charm brings the two together, and replaces the ideal of monumentality that had prevailed in the 1st half of the century.

The head of Deva shown here reflects the innovative spirit of the style. Everything in it illustrates this spirit. The smiling grace of the plump face, the high, full, and almost sensual lips, the slight curve of the nose, the outline of the eyes and of the eyebrows all break with the tradition. Even the more naturalistic treatment of the short beard, and the arrangement of the small loops in the style of an ascetic's hair mark a total change of orientation.

This new aesthetic, which is in total contrast with the one that had begun its evolution early in the IXth century, does not seem only due to the intelligent copying of a remote past. It evokes too much of the gentleness of Javanese bas-reliefs, especially those of Prambanan,[1] for this to be only accidental. And it would be very surprising if the Javanese ideal were solely rediscovered through the inspiration drawn from the Khmer models of the VIIth and VIIIth centuries, even though these might have been originally influenced by Java. . . . Whatever the puzzle, and it does seem to be a very complex one, the head of Deva in the Phnom Penh Museum illustrates well enough all the new elements contributed by the *Banteay Srei style*.

This turning point is so important to the development of Khmer art that for a long time one hesitated to give the monument its true date, 967 A.D. In an effort to reason that such elaboration and originality characterize the terminal phase of an art, and on the acceptance of an inadequate study of the inscriptions, it was believed the temple was built in the XIVth century. But if Banteay Srei seems to break almost entirely with the traditions immediately preceding it, a break more apparent than real, it still heralds the art that will unfold in the XIth century, linking the innovations with a gradual return to traditional formulas.

---

[1]The Prambanan, or Loro Djonggrang monuments are generally attributed to approximately the mid-IXth century (known as the Central Javanese Period). (Ed.)

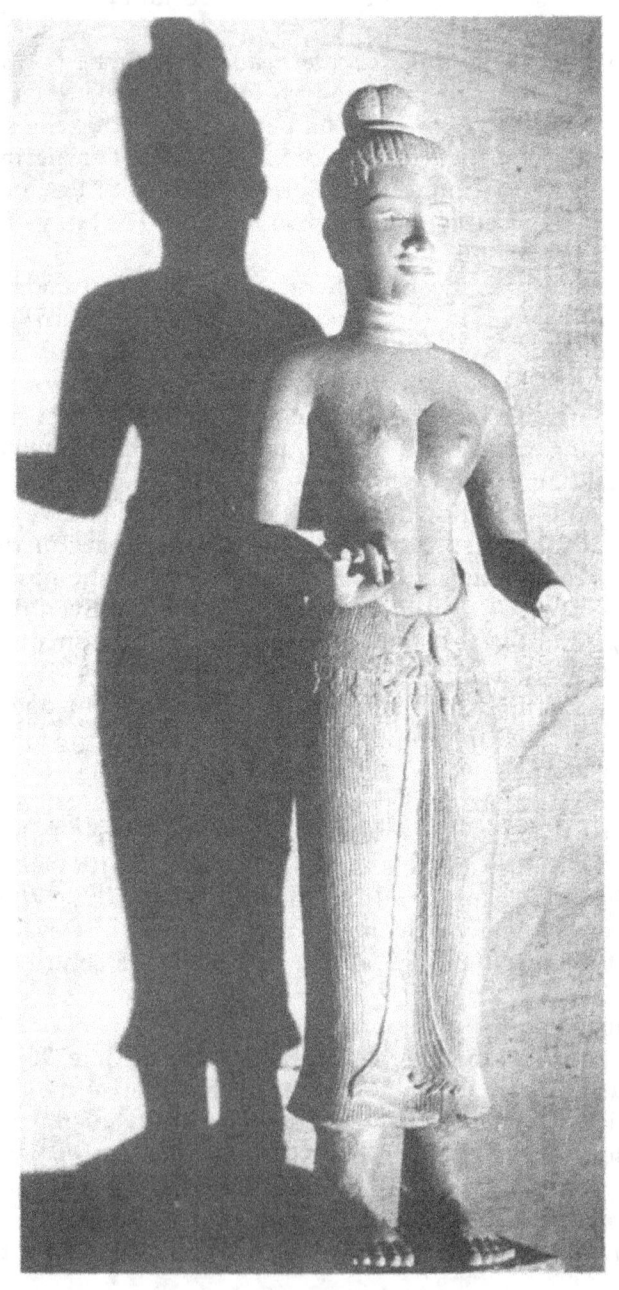

FIGURE XIV

FIGURE XIV

Feminine Divinity (B-52, 9)

Sandstone (H. 1 m.—39 3/8") Prasat Trapeang Totung Thngay (Siem Reap)
XIth century

While this divinity is most likely Lakshmī, Vishnu's *śakti*, her identity cannot be determined with certitude due to the absence of attributes. But the quest for grace inherited from Banteay Srei and the ideal of slenderness very peculiar to the art of the XIth century, are remarkably characteristic of the *Bàphuon style*.

The sculptor has achieved here an overall effect of suppleness and graceful slenderness by elongating the forms and giving the statue a slight *hanchement*, which, moreover, is very feminine. This is contrary to the long-accepted opinion that regards frontality and hieratical posture as the absolute rule for the statuary that followed the middle of the IXth century.

The craftsmanship is particularly delicate in most works of a style which, being much less in pursuit of architectural aspect than of a rather naturalistic refinement, is much nearer us than the ideal of mighty power that had prevailed from the Prah Kô style to the Koh Ker style. The remaining hand is remarkably delicate, and even the feet, the weak point of Khmer statuary, are treated quite successfully here. The gentle and very feminine face still shows in the outline of the lips some of the sensuality that had appeared at Banteay Srei. We also note the finely braided hair gathered into a high and elaborate chignon and the dimple on the chin, both features being characteristic of the style.

Following a technique which also belongs to the *Bàphuon style*, the eyes are hollowed; they were possibly meant to receive inlaid pupils, but since no discoveries have supported this hypothesis up to now, the technique may perhaps be compared to the one Roman sculptors practiced for some time.

The very simple garment, generously revealing the abdomen, is derived from the one that Banteay Srei, inspired by models of the VIIth and VIIIth century, brought back into fashion. But as it links here the simplicity of Banteay Srei with the pleating of the 1st half of the Xth century, it is rather a combination of the two styles. Also, the pleating has become very fine, and gives the fabric a new buoyancy. The front panel of the skirt is folded over and its lower part spreads out in the shape of a "fish-tail" which seems to be an invention of the *Bàphuon style* (fig. J). The skirt is held up by a twisted knot we see at the upper edge. The single knot is generally on the left side; sometimes the knot is double. (Ed.)

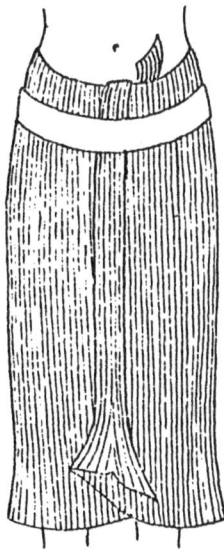

fig. J

"Fish-tail" drapery of feminine garment
Bàphuon style

An almost excessive elongation of the forms, and a certain propensity to femininity could have led this art on the downward path to mannerism and affectation. It would seem that the artists sensed this and towards the end of the century they reacted against this trend. In the Angkor Vat period this reaction led to a radical change of orientation that renewed the formulas and instilled the statuary with a new ideal.

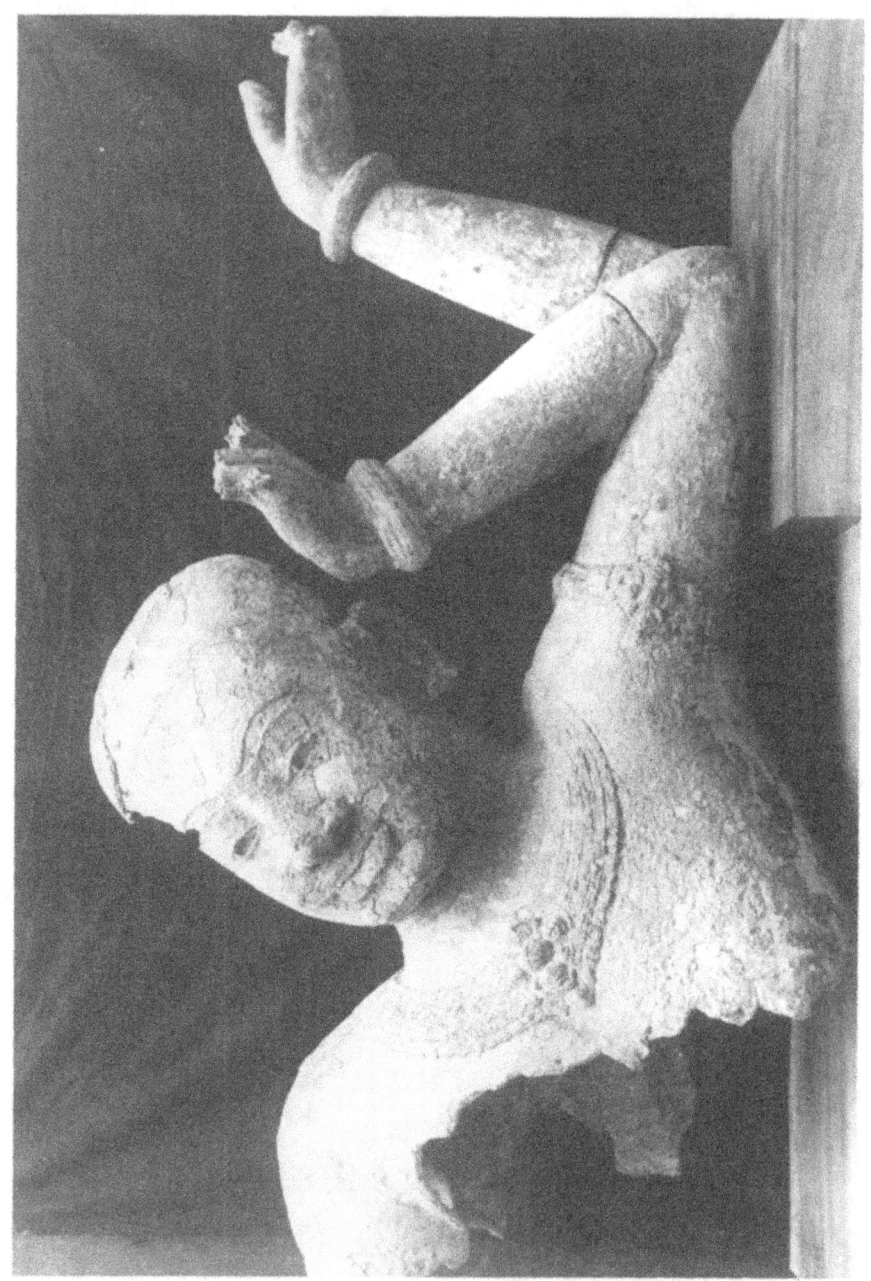

FIGURE XV

FIGURE XV

Bust of Reclining Vishnu (E/1-30, 17)

Bronze (H. 1 m. 14—44 7/8") Western Mébon of Angkor
Approximately mid-XIth century

This is undoubtedly one of the master works of Khmer statuary, as much for its beauty as for the technical tour de force that represents the casting of such a large statue.

It once roused the admiration of the Chinese envoy Zhou Daguan who traveled through Cambodia in 1296, and left a most valuable and often savory account of his stay in the Khmer capital. Our writer, however, did not seem much concerned with iconography nor with orientation, since he believed this to be an image of the reclining Buddha, and placed it east of Angkor whereas it was to its west.

Recognizable by his four arms, this is actually Vishnu reclining on the Serpent of Eternity *Śesha* (or *Ananta*), borne by the waves of the Ocean. During the interval that separates two cosmic periods (*kalpa*), Vishnu thus falls asleep while a golden lotus bearing Brahmā, the creator of the worlds, emerges from his navel. At the dawn of each era Vishnu incarnates himself into a new *avatāra* in order to defeat the evil forces and rescue the created beings. The episode of Vishnu's sleep was often represented in India as it was in Cambodia, but sculptures in the round are very rare. A bronze of such considerable size is a unique piece, far removed from a certain mannerism that one might fear was latent in the divinity of Figure XIV.

The god's serene grandeur asserts itself at first glance, and the accuracy of proportions helps us overlook the colossal dimensions of the statue. Nothing in it overpowers us: the gentleness of the face, the beauty of the hands transcending their maimed condition, all make this a deeply human work.

The sumptuousness of the bronze's adornment already foretells the trends that will unfold in the Angkor Vat style. The figure wore a diadem, now unfortunately gone, that was assembled with tenons or rivets required by casting. The moustache, the beard confined to the chin, the eyebrows, and the pupils were set in and possibly made of a more precious metal.

The casting of a statue of such importance implies that Khmer bronze casters possessed a mastery that cannot be stressed enough. In the West, large statues were not cast again until the XVth century, after an interruption of some twelve centuries. Until the Western Mébon Vishnu was discovered in 1936, one only knew small size bronzes in Cambodia or, judging by the rare fragments found (hands or feet), of human size at best. Must the Western Mébon Vishnu stand as a unique work or is it the lone surviving witness of the skills of Khmer bronze casters? Owing to the present state of discoveries, we cannot answer. But bronze, a precious metal coveted over the centuries, has all too often tempted the greed of plunderers in the past to give us much of a chance of someday resolving this problem.

Nota. Recent discoveries (especially the head of a colossal Bodhisattva, Ban Tahnot in the Khorat plateau, Thailand; the bull Nandin, Tûol Kuhea, Cambodia), and new research (statues of lions, of the elephant Airāvata, and of several *dvārapāla* now kept in Mandalay, Burma), prove that the art of monumental bronze casting was also fully mastered by the Khmers in the VIIIth century (*style of*

Kompong Prah), and at the end of the XIIth and in the beginning of the XIIIth centuries (*Bàyon style*).[1]

---

[1]J. Boisselier, "Notes sur l'art du bronze dans l'ancien Cambodge . . .," *Artibus Asiae* XXIX (1966), pp. 275–334.

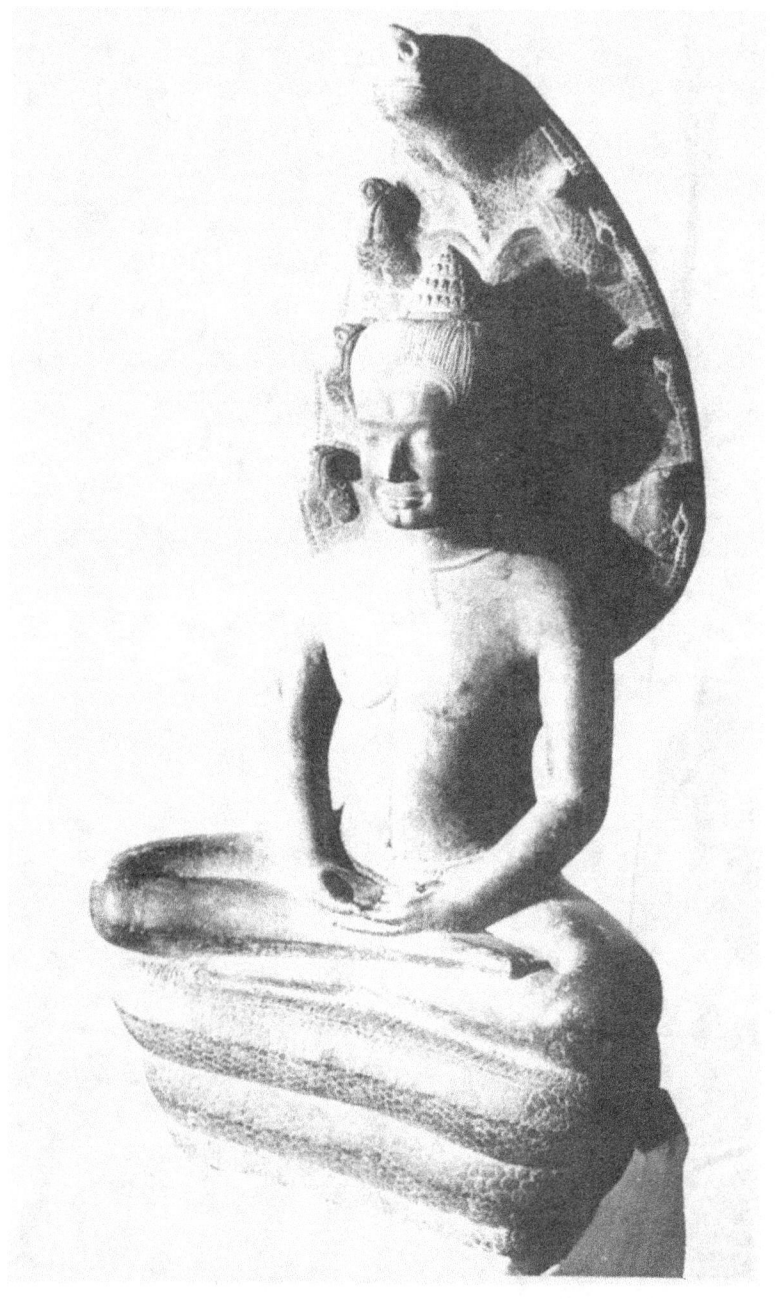

FIGURE XVI

FIGURE XVI

Buddha Sheltered by the Nāga (B-10, 20)

Sandstone (H. 1 m. 15—45 1/4") Peam Cheang Plantation (Kompong Thom)
XIth century

This statue is as remarkable for its execution as for its state of preservation. It marks the moment when the type of the meditating Buddha sheltered by a *nāga*, which became so popular, tends to assert itself. One is familiar with the event illustrated here, so dear to Khmer art: in the course of the seven weeks that followed the attainment of Full Enlightenment, torrential rains were unleashed during a whole week. *Mucilinda*, king of the serpent-Genies, came out of the ground and protected the Master's meditation with his body's coils and his outspread hood.

The new images of the Buddha which reappeared towards the middle of the Xth century were influenced by the aesthetics of the more abundant Hindu imagery of the period. This "contamination" explains the unexpected headdress of the Predestined One: instead of being made up of the traditional spiral curls, his hair is gathered in neatly braided tresses and a conical "coif," actually a *mukuta*, covers the *ushnīsha*. Such details are indeed far removed from classical iconography. . . . Moreover, although properly speaking this statue is unadorned, we notice that the *mukuta* and the hairline are edged by a finely engraved decoration that could be regarded as a first discreet attempt at showing adornment.

The bust which appears to be naked, and the completely free arms make it difficult to imagine a garment covering the torso, but the slight protrusion at the edge of the neck, and a furrow that emphasizes the center of the chest help us imagine that, in a fashion as personal as it is illogical, the sculptor has indicated a garment clinging to the body.

The fineness of the face and the elegant nose are quite unusual, but the dimple in the center of the chin is very peculiar to the *Bàphuon style;* so are the simply incised outlines of the eyes which occur more frequently than the hollowed pupils we noticed in Figure XIV.

The body is very soberly modeled but it is nevertheless admirably accurate. We cannot stress enough the artist's assurance in conveying the relaxation of the arms so befitting the lack of physical tension meditation demands. In later times other statues of the Buddha attained a more intense interior life, but only a few were to regain the genuineness of attitude this one has.

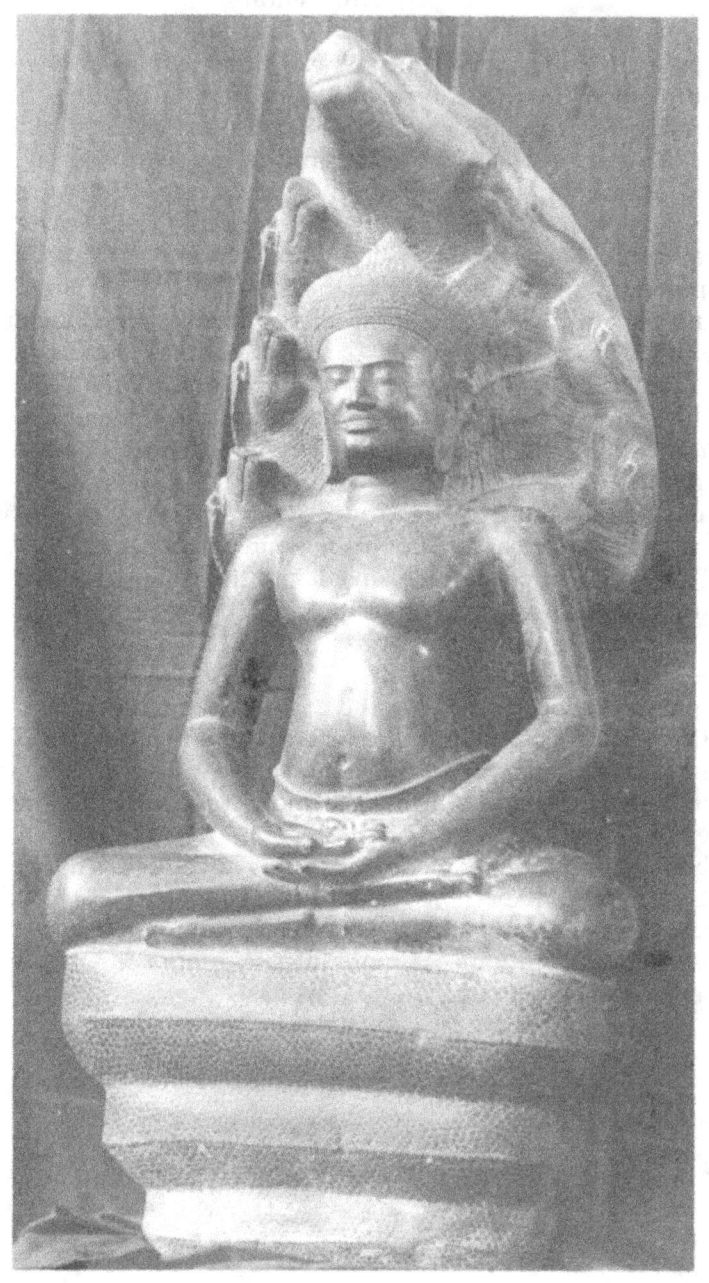

FIGURE XVII

FIGURE XVII

Adorned Buddha Sheltered by the Nāga (B-10, 7)

Waxed sandstone (H. 0 m. 87—34 1/4") From a cave in the Sisophon region
First half of the XIIth century

Like the Buddha in Figure XVI, this one is shown meditating, seated on the coils of the *nāga*-King Mucilinda. The same moment in the life of the Master is illustrated even though here he appears endowed with regal emblems: a diadem and a *mukuta*.

Such adornment may seem inappropriate for the Buddha who, after renouncing all worldly wealth, had actually stripped himself of regalia in order to become a simple wandering monk. The considerable importance adorned images acquired in the Indochinese peninsula was brought out in G. Cœdès's work. A study by Paul Mus[1] has demonstrated the doctrinal significance of this rather unexpected convention, but one which was attested to in India at quite an early date; the author underscores that. . . "The worship of the Buddha performed according to the royal ceremonial derives from the earliest conceptions wherein the new spirit of Buddhism asserted itself." Originally, these images no doubt evoked an aspect of the transcendental Buddha as much as the historical Buddha in the guise of the Universal Monarch. In Southeast Asia this assimilation does not seem to have prevailed until the advance of the Theravāda doctrine. It seems founded on the great victories of the Buddha: his victory over Māra, the enticing god who binds beings to everything that is perishable and vain; the conquest of the *Bodhi*, the Enlightenment, his ultimate victory considered to be the "Unperishable Monarchy"; and lastly, the reputed apocryphal one over Jambupati, the sovereign who made undue claims to Universal Monarchy.

The work reflects the qualities and the trends of the statuary of the *Angkor Vat style:* frontal and hieratical posture, simplification of volumes, and extreme care in the execution of details.

The face is serene, but it does not have the gleam of interior life or the feeling of compassion that will only appear a little later in the Bàyon period. It has also lost some of the charm and gentleness it still had in the Bàphuon period that was inherited from Banteay Srei. Even though the eyes are closed, which is unusual for the period, it seems that the artist was more in pursuit of a majestic ideal and of superficial beatitude than trying to achieve any depth of feeling.

It should also be noted that just as in the Buddha of Figure XVI, the hair is plaited. As for the diadem and the *mukuta*, they are simply the royal emblems that we see all alike, in images of Vishnu or worn by Sūryavarman II in the bas-reliefs of Angkor Vat. The torso appears completely naked, and any recollection of the garment that could still be presumed in the Peam Cheang Buddha is now gone.

When Khmer iconography represents the Buddha in the royal aspect, it draws directly from the repertory of contemporaneous models. This trend has perpetuated itself up to now, and recent images show the Buddha with the very same costume the Kings wear on Coronation day, complete with the *mukuta*, boots, and shoulder armour.

---

[1] Paul Mus, "Le Buddha paré" (*Bulletin de l'Ecole française d'Extrême-Orient* XXVIII, p.153 ff., Hanoi, 1928).

the Kings wear on Coronation day, complete with the *mukuta*, boots, and shoulder armour.

One cannot fail to notice the profound aesthetic change that took place since the Bàphuon style: forms have become stockier, the face is squarer; and not unlike what they were in the beginning of the Xth century, the orbital ridges are sharp again. The Banteay Srei ideal that still inspired the art of the XIth century, but that was in danger of being overpowered by mannerism as its original vitality turned into formulas, has now given way to the more architectural conceptions of the era that saw the birth of the most extensive and most perfect temples: Angkor Vat and Beng Mealea. . . .

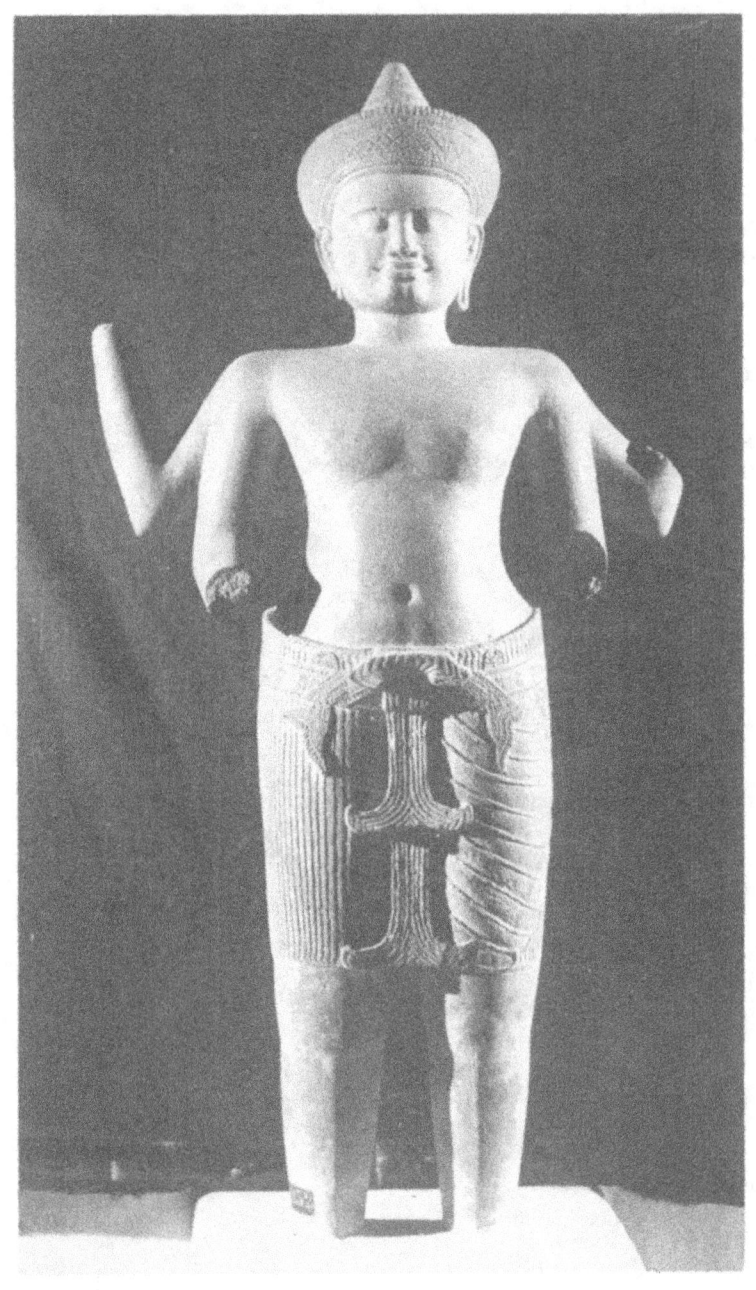

FIGURE XVIII

FIGURE XVIII

Vishnu (B-30, 7)

Sandstone (H. 1 m. 01—39 3/4") Vat Knat (Siem Reap)
First half of XIIth century

Despite the absence of the attributes which alone would make possible a definite identification of this statue, one can consider this to be an image of Vishnu on account of the four arms and of the headgear made up of the diadem and conical *mukuta*. We saw the same headgear on the Buddha in Figure XVII, and have mentioned that representations of Sūryavarman II were also decked out with it. Here we find it worn by Vishnu, the one and only god of the Hindu pantheon who can claim the title of Universal Monarch.

The work is properly characteristic of the *Angkor Vat style* whose statuary breaks off entirely, though not abruptly and with continuous impetus, with the traditions of the Bàphuon period. As against the slightly feminine grace that was held in honor in the XIth century, this style returns to frontality and hieratical posture.

The forms are massive: the shoulders are wide and straight, and the square face recalls a little the types of the 1st half of the Xth century. While they remain full, the lips have lost their sensuality; the orbital ridges are unbroken, barely sinuous, and almost sharp; the bulging eyes look myopic; the stylized beard, which in the Bàphuon period was no more than a bow-shaped outline confined to the chin, has vanished altogether.

The costume, likewise, recalls aspects predating Banteay Srei, but the "anchor falls" are quite different, and they come down very low; lying flat on the left hip, the "pocket-fold" is completely stylized (fig. K), and often it is even eliminated. The belt is constantly embellished so as to become an element of the adornment.

Except for the Koh Ker style, the statuary of the Angkor Vat period gave bejeweled adornments their greatest prominence. The belt is always ornate, the presence of the diadem and of the *mukuta* is constant, feminine images nearly always wear a necklace, bracelets, and anklets. Moreover, the characteristics of this adornment assure that the bas-reliefs and the statuary of Angkor Vat are contemporaneous, for apart from aesthetic considerations which are often difficult to bring out, they are the only link.

Bas-reliefs and sculptures in the round never showed an absolute sameness, and in the art of Angkor Vat they became completely disassociated. The bas-reliefs show costumes with long flowing flaps that derive from the transformation of the Bàphuon drapery. But held back by technical difficulties the statuary could not adopt this fashion, and reverted to the old forms of drapery.

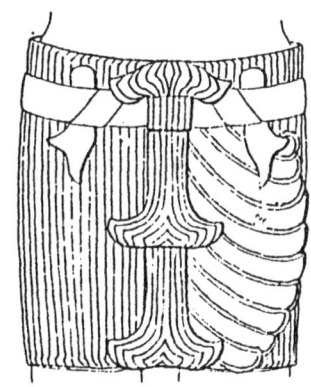

fig. K
"Anchor falls" and "Pocket-fold"
drapery of Angkor Vat style male
garment

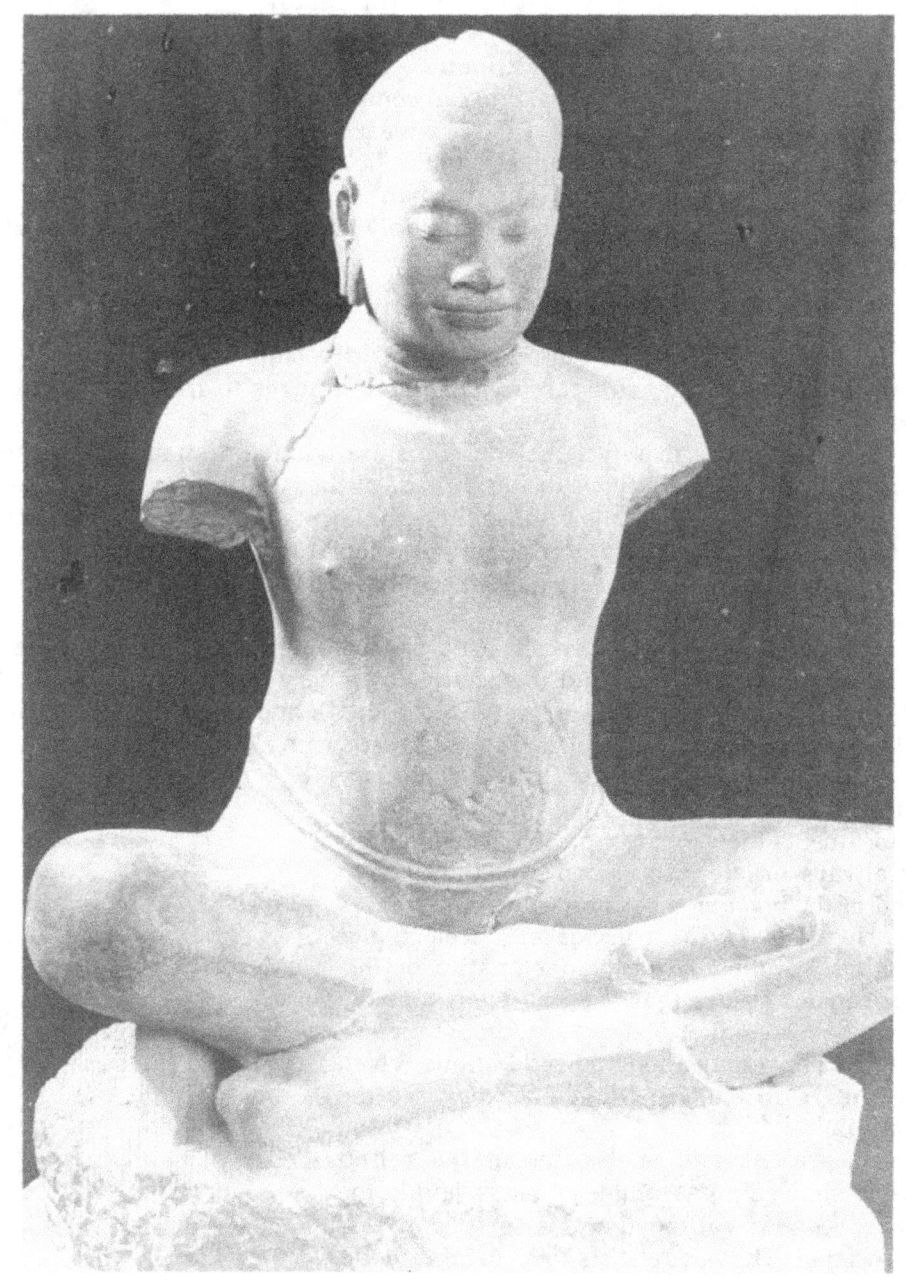

FIGURE XIX

FIGURE XIX

Jayavarman VII (?) (B-19, 1)

Sandstone (H. 1 m. 13—44 15/32") Krol Romeas (Angkor Thom)
End of XIIth to beginning of XIIIth century

This statue is one of the most powerful works of all Khmer art. It represents an unknown personage whose various traits have led George Cœdès, to whom we owe our knowledge of Jayavarman VII's life and work,[1] to take it for an image of the great king.

It is a fact that the identity of the monarch can hardly be questioned in some bas-reliefs scenes from the Bàyon and Banteay Chmar. He appears there with the same features as here, and in his study of Jayavarman VII George Cœdès has written:

Physically he was a rather portly man, with heavy features, who wore his hair pulled up and forming a small chignon on top of his head. All these features, which clearly appear in the bas-reliefs, can also be seen in two statues, one found at Angkor Thom, the other, which came from Phimai near Korat [sic], preserved in Bangkok. Although I am not absolutely positive, I suggest we recognize in these two images, obviously representing the same personage, two images of Jayavarman VII.

We side most willingly with the learned opinion of G. Cœdès because we believe we can support it with some additional arguments.

This statue was clearly inspired by an actual model. The artist has sought an impression of strength, without fearing to translate his model's corpulence through a totally unconventional rendering of volumes. The face may be the most thoroughly Khmer face ever sculpted, and the features' slight dissymmetry seems to reveal the portrait.

The very peculiar appearance of the smooth hair topped by a small chignon, which is still intact in the Bangkok Museum statue, does not befit a divinity. Conversely, as G. Cœdès has emphasized, it recalls the images in the bas-reliefs. Finally, although the loss of the arms prevents us from being specific, the attitude, judging by the fractures, does not seem to be one of the traditional gestures of Buddhist divinities. The figure was probably making the offertory gesture or was at prayer and the legs crossed in the Indian fashion could only be conceived for a very high-ranking personality.

The beauty, the power, and the simplicity of the work speak for themselves. Having heard all too often that the art of the Bàyon sacrificed form for the sole benefit of expression, one cannot fail to notice that the exceptional qualities of this face were not the sculptor's only concern. The body is modeled with an accuracy and restraint that belong only to great art and evoke the style of A. Maillol. We must also mention the outline of the knees and the true accuracy of the musculature of the legs. Only the treatment of the foot seems a little awkward, but even this flaw

---

[1] George Cœdès, "The Last Great King of Angkor, Jayavarman VII," pp. 84 ff. in *Angkor, an Introduction*, translated and edited by Emily Floyd Gardiner, Oxford University Press, Hong Kong 1963; "Les statues du roi khmer Jayavarman VII" (*Compte-rendus*, Académie des Inscriptions et Belles-Lettres, 4-7-1958, pp. 218 ff.).

indicates a direct observation of the model; in this position the foot is likely to appear deformed. Here we are nowhere near the stylization unrelated to true movement that was adopted for all the statues seated in the Indian fashion. In any case, this flaw can take nothing away from the extraordinary vitality, both spiritual and physical, that animates this œuvre, one of the most masterful sculptures of all time.

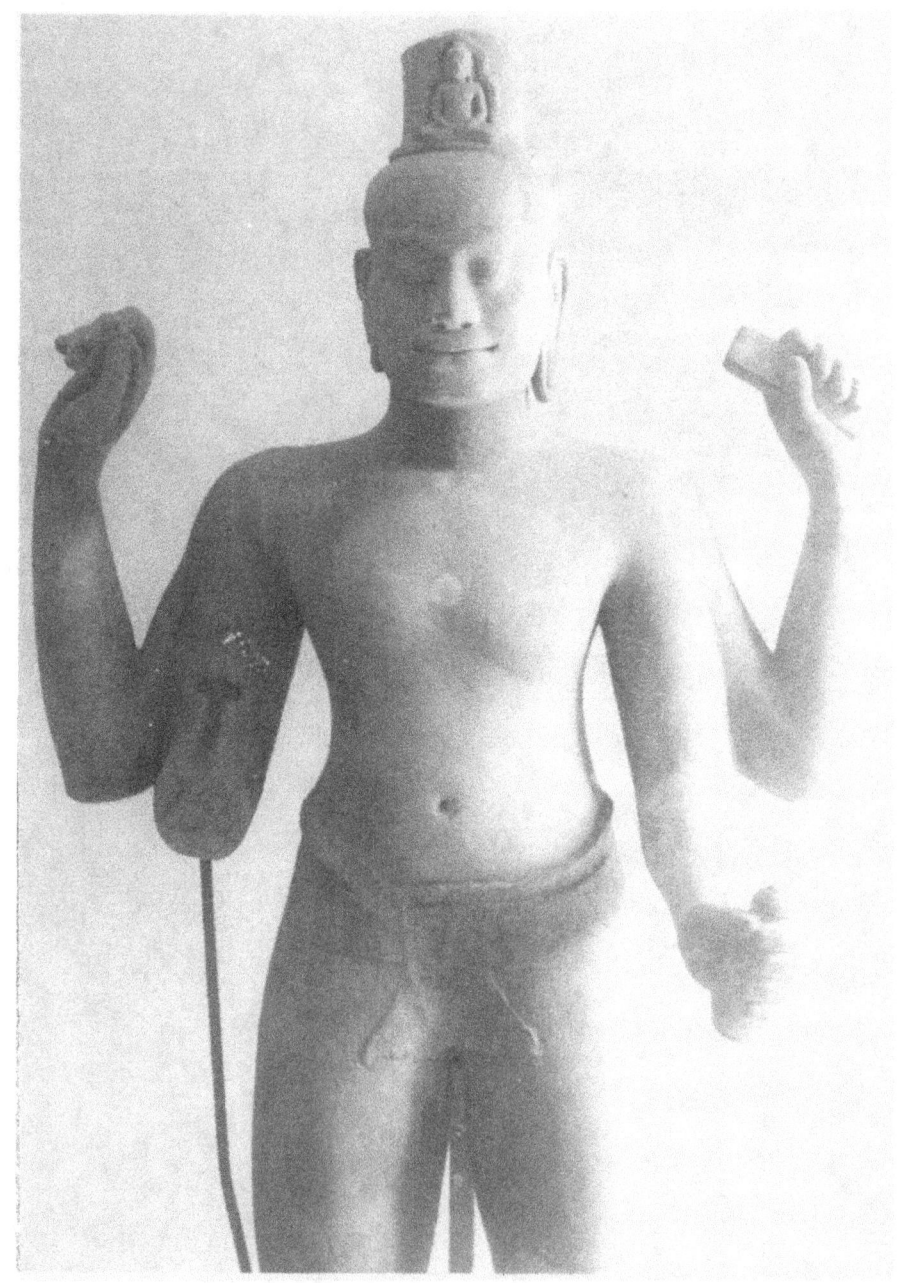

FIGURE XX

FIGURE XX

Lokeśvara (B-11, 5)

Sandstone (H. 2 m. 12—83 15/32") Gate of the Dead (Angkor Thom)
End of the XIIth to beginning of XIIIth century

Lokeśvara was one of the most popular divinities of the Mahāyānist pantheon during the reign of Jayavarman VII. In this image he appears with four arms, the aspect in which he is most often seen.

He is the compassionate Bodhisattva, the spiritual son of the Dhyāni-Buddha *Amitābha* whose image he bears in his headdress. Protector from all perils, healer, giving assistance to all, Lokeśvara was the ideal model after whom Jayavarman wished to shape his life, as evidenced by the epigraphy of the monarch's reign.

Lokeśvara's personality is an extremely complex one and his aspects are most diversified. When he has four arms, we notice that he has the same attributes as Brahmā: the ambrosial flask, the book, the rosary (the only ones remaining here), and the pink lotus.

As in the case of all divinities of the Mahāyānist pantheon, Lokeśvara wears the same garment as a Hindu divinity, a highly simplified garment which characterizes the Bàyon period sculptures in the round (fig. L). The sculptor seems to have been inspired by the same royal model as for the preceding work. It has the same corpulence of a mature but strongly built man. All of his musculature points to a man who must have been well trained in all sport activities in his youth, and this trait is in accord with what we know of the sovereign. And yet, the face is more idealized so as to better suit a Bodhisattva.

The closed eyes help evoke the compassion which is the spiritual and artistic ideal of the Bàyon period, and one which responds so well to Lokeśvara's personality. The smiling lips are almost parted, which is unusual, and convey an impression of radiance where can be found some of the "brilliance" of which the texts speak.

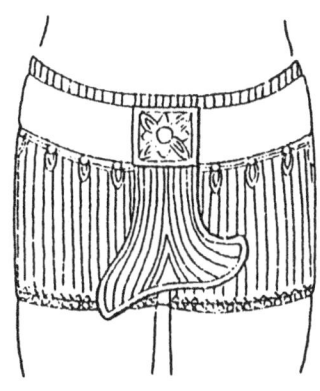

fig. L
"Anchor fall" drapery of Bàyon
style male statuary

The execution technique is worthy of study. Indeed, it will be noted that each of the arms, as is true of the legs at mid-calf, was assembled with the help of a double "T" element. This is not due to repairs made later, but is a device called for by the statue's dimensions which required a sandstone block of considerable size. As one could not be found, the sculptor had to assemble the limbs by positioning them with carefully adjusted sandstone anchors, following a standard method used in Khmer construction. The system's lack of solidity caused the statue's disrepair; we did not find its three forearms until 1950.

The difficulty in securing large homogeneous sandstone blocks is only one explanation for the mediocre shape of so many statues in this style. Good quality sandstone became scarce in the Bàyon period; the builders had to make use of a softer sandstone for their constructions, scale the monuments to a smaller size, and increase the use of laterite for all the least important parts of the monuments. Sculptors, too, had to make the best of the same poor quality sandstone, fragile and ill-suited for polishing. In an effort to assure the longevity of their work they over-enlarged the lower limbs, and left the forms almost in their rough state so as to avoid putting too great a stress on the stone during shaping. In spite of these precautions, which do not explain all of the frequent mediocrities of the style, few statues have survived unscathed. Broken up, eroded by rain, they are the ones that have suffered the most from the ravages of time. Even the most important works, for which the sandstone was selected with the greatest care, have not fared much better, as the skin of the sandstone burst in patches.

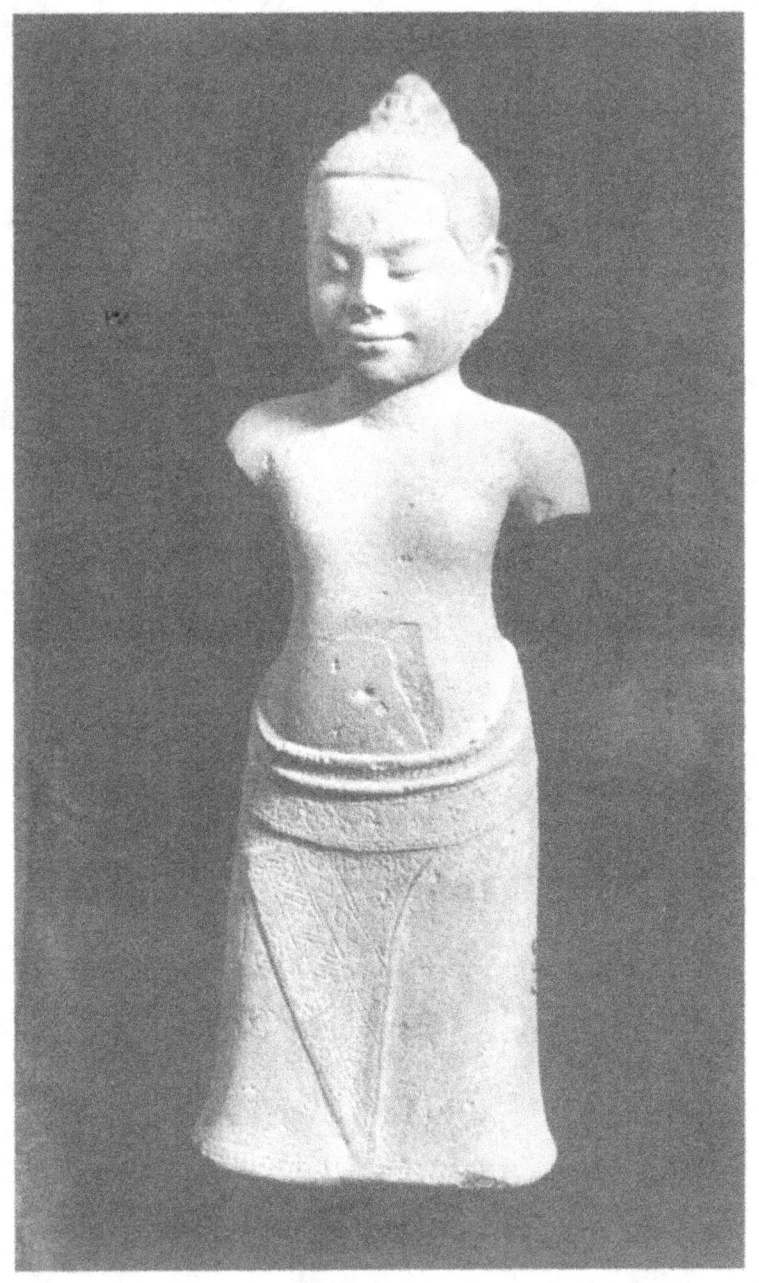

FIGURE XXI

FIGURE XXI

Tārā (B-12, 4)

Sandstone (H. 0 m. 735—28 15/16") From the brush area north of Angkor Thom
End of XIIth or beginning of XIIIth century

It seems that this mutilated statue, deprived of the attributes which could have made her identification possible with some certitude, should be called Tārā rather than Prajñāpāramitā as was suggested at first. The fact that it undeniably evokes a portrait, and of a child to boot, does not change the problem; first of all, it is a statue of a Mahāyānist divinity, this being established by the image of a Buddha in her headdress. Tārā, the "Saviouress," whose number and variety of representations are described in the texts, holds a position of considerable importance in Mahāyānist iconography. In Khmer art her chignon is always conical whereas that of Lokeśvara, whose assistant or companion she is, is cylindrical. Certain aspects of the divinity, which depict her with multiple heads and arms, are only represented in high reliefs and by a few bronze statuettes in Cambodia. In sculpture in the round we only know her in the human form, generally holding the lotus and the book.

The image here is unexpected because it represents Tārā with unusual features. The statue is unquestionably that of a child; the large size of the head in relation to the body, the overall forms, the underdeveloped breasts and the modelling of the face are those of a young girl, about ten years old, in whose features one is surprised to recognize the divinity. . . . George Cœdès was the first to underline the importance of personal cults in Cambodia.[1] Statues could represent living people "whose essence they were supposed to contain, that is to say, their vital principle." After their death, the inscriptions endlessly plead for the strict observance of the rites by the subsequent monarchs so as to enable the soul of the deceased to return and dwell in the statue for a while. This is likely to be the image of a young Princess of the blood who had died prematurely and was honored with deification ceremonies of the type we know could also be bestowed upon some Princes and their comrades in arms for wartime exploits.

The statue wears the same garment as all the other feminine statues of the Bàyon period: a very simple skirt, where a spray of carved flowerets has replaced the pleating, adorned in front by the overlap of a large flap (figs. M-a, & M-b), and held in place by a wide finely chiseled belt.

The headdress, made up of finely plaited tresses, is a highly developed and stylized recollection of the hair-style that had appeared in the Banteay Srei period.

The facial expression is infantile and meditative and echoes well the physical ideal of the style.[2] In a face that was meant more to smile than for deep thoughts, the artist has engraved a slightly pert expression that curls up the corners of the lips. It appears a little sad, perhaps in pain, and deeply poignant.

---

[1] G. Cœdès, "Personal Cults," pp. 22 ff. in *Angkor, an Introduction*, translated and edited by Emily Floyd Gardiner, Oxford University Press, Hong Kong 1963.

[2] J. Boisselier, "Reflexions sur l'art de Jayavarman VII," *Bulletin de la Société des Etudes indochinoises*, Saigon, *Nouvelle Série*, t. XXVII, 3 (1952), pp. 261 ff.

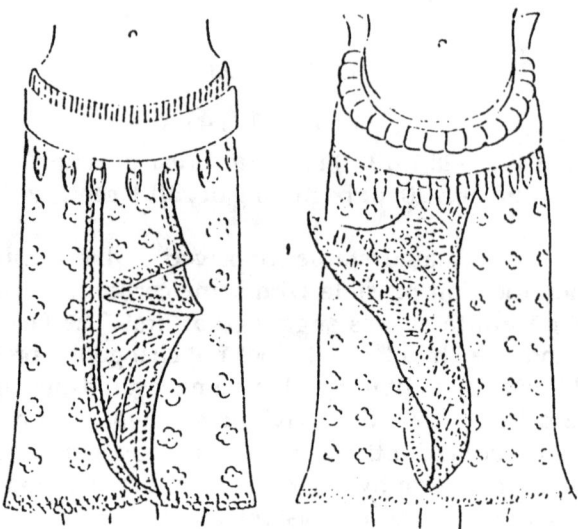

figs. M-a and M-b
Draperies of feminine garments, Bàyon style

While it seems difficult to specify which particular aspect of Tārā this statue represents, it must nevertheless be said that the *Bàyon style* probably did not entirely create this type, but that it rather used certain themes of the Mahāyānist texts in an original way. When the texts indicate how Tārā should be represented when she is to be invoked or portrayed, they often specify that she seems "to be sixteen," and much more seldom, "twelve years of age." This last characteristic seems to have been held to here.

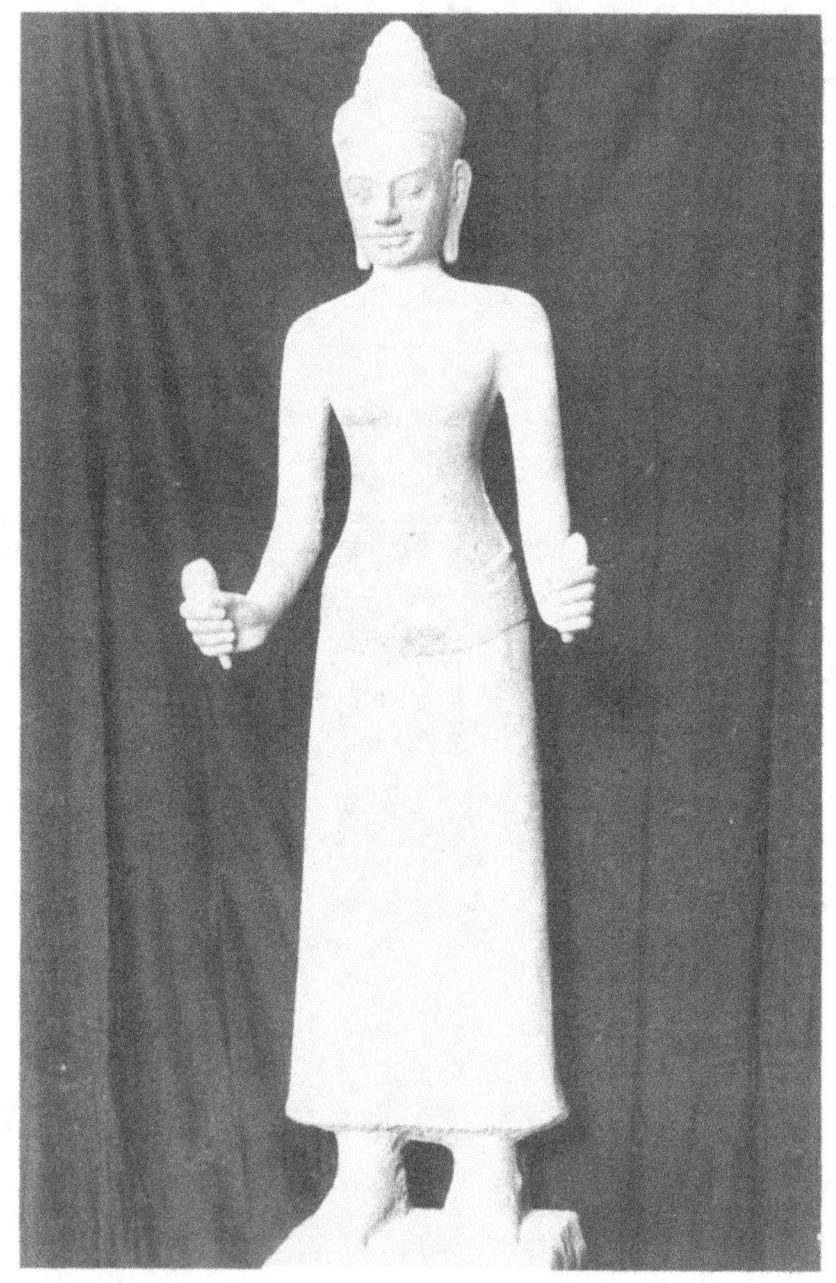

FIGURE XXII

FIGURE XXII

Lakshmī (B-32, 10)

Sandstone (H. 1 m. 84—72 7/16") Prah Kô (Rolûoh)
End of XIIth to beginning of XIIIth century

Lakshmī, Vishnu's *śakti*, is recognized here by the attributes she holds: a lotus bud in each hand. These two lotus buds and the absence of the Dhyāni-Buddha in her chignon are the only differences between her images and those of Tārā and of Prajñāpāramitā.

As it happens, whenever a religion becomes predominant, it affects the whole of the contemporaneous statuary. When Hinduism was predominant, Buddhist images inherited some traits from Brahmanic images. Now, at the height of the Mahāyānist mood, the fashion is set by statues of divinities of the newly imposed cult: it is the same attitude, the same costume, the same face, the same hair arrangement. Only the attributes of a given cult are unchangeable. But one noteworthy difference characterizes the two types of statuary and reflects the different spirit that animates them: the eyes of Buddhist images are always either closed or half-closed; conversely, Hindu images keep their eyes open. The law tolerates only rare exceptions that mostly deal with images of poor workmanship, works of provincial ateliers or representations of ascetics for whom closed eyes are the traditional rule.

This being said, the Prah Kô Lakshmī shows all the characteristics of feminine statuary of the *Bàyon style*. Totally breaking off from the traditions that had been maintained until then, the forms seem lank; the shoulders are narrow, the breasts small, the hips wide.... The long thin face is likewise very peculiar to the style. In this statue we find once more the wish to evoke a specific personage. Previously we have emphasized the style's propensity for portraiture, and here, as with Botticelli but in a different spirit, the forms evoke those of a sick lady, most likely consumptive.... And we learn from history that King Jayavarman VII's first Queen, a very pious, perfect wife, probably died young. The King then married her older sister, also a very pious lady, one of the most learned of her day and one to whom we owe the most beautiful inscriptions of the reign. In one of the inscriptions she states that she had images of her dead sister set up everywhere. Claiming no more than that this is a hypothesis, we are somewhat tempted to recognize the deceased Queen's features idealized in the great many feminine images that share so many common points. In any case, and whatever her actual identity might be, the wish to evoke physically a given personality seems evident.

Prah Kô, the statue's provenance, calls for additional remarks. The monument was actually consecrated in 879, and unquestionably, the statue belongs to the Bàyon style. Almost every sanctuary received repeated consecrations, and if in this instance the stylistic differences are very sharp, the example shows the caution that should be exercised when trying to date statues. In most cases, the statues postdate the original monument, but it can also happen that a pious gesture, made at some undetermined time has assembled earlier statues in a sanctuary of a later date.

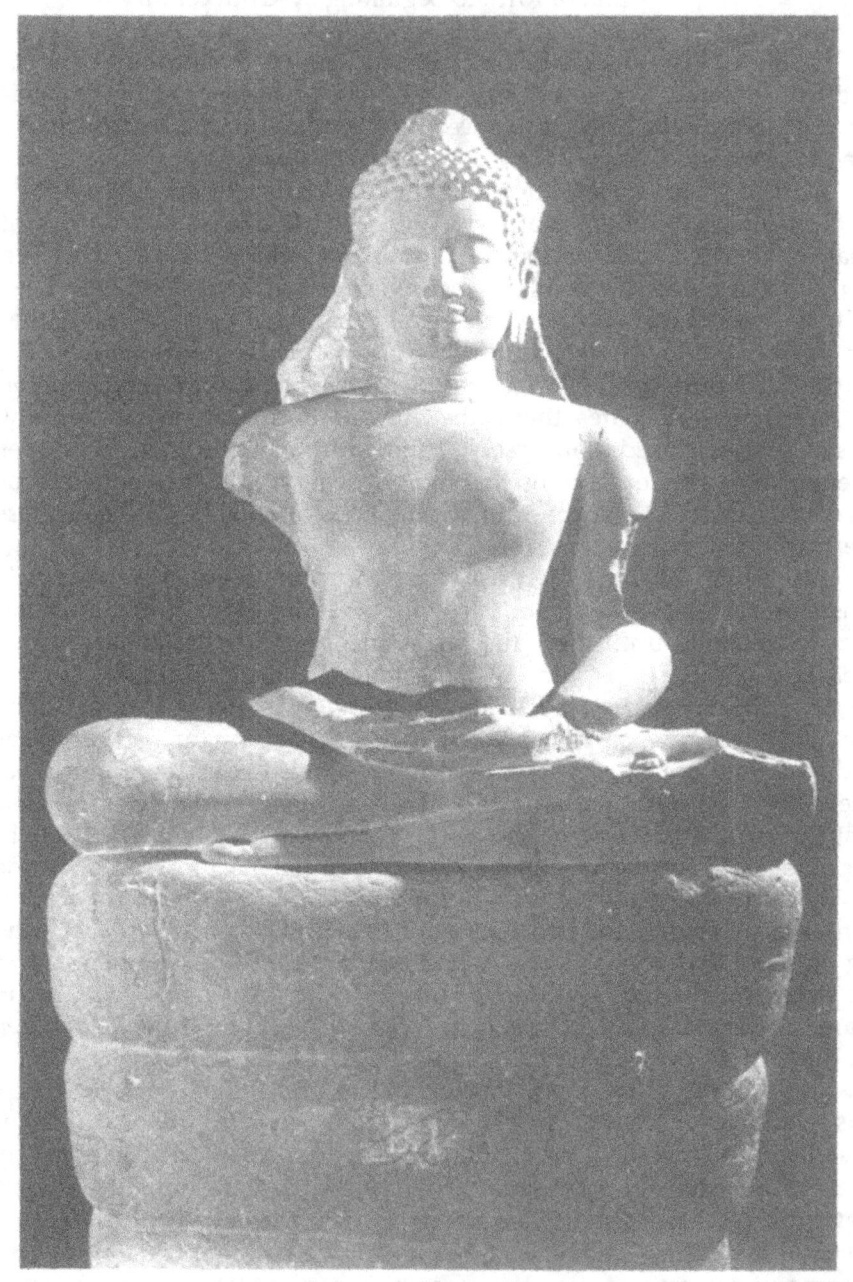

FIGURE XXIII

FIGURE XXIII

Buddha Sheltered by the Nāga (B-10, 3)
Sandstone (H. 0 m. 93—36 19/32") Bàyon (Angkor Thom)
XIIIth century

This is the famous Buddha known as the "Commaille" Buddha, found in 1913 by the first Curator of the Angkor Monuments. Thanks to a study Alfred Foucher devoted to it in the very year of its discovery, the work can probably claim the credit for contributing most to drawing attention to the qualities of Khmer statuary.

The Buddha is shown here at the same moment of his life as in Figures XVI and XVII. But this time he appears without any adornment and the bust seems to be completely naked. A garment that covers the left shoulder and leaves the right shoulder bare is nevertheless suggested by the solid area that joins the left arm and the body. Due to a convention we have not had occasion to mention yet, it seems that this stylization is the end result of a progressive simplification which, in the Bàyon period, sometimes indicated discreetly the upper part of the garment by means of a protrusion near the wrist, and of a slight outline across the chest.

This is a highly stylized work, somewhat lifeless perhaps, yet filled with serenity and gentleness, and of undisputed stateliness. But it no longer reflects the interior life and communion with beings that the Bàyon style had known how to translate. Seemingly, these feelings have been stilled. The classical qualities, in the Western sense of the word, are evident, but they belong to a declining classicism that bears the seeds of some intellectual dryness as do so many Hellenistic works. This is the time when only the art of the sculptor makes one forget the latent flaws that soon turned into clichés.

The "Commaille" Buddha had been made into a prototype of Khmer Buddhas "seated on the Nāga" whose origin might have been the old, traditionally Buddhist Mōn kingdom of Dvāravatī. This was on account of a few traits that recall a little the aesthetics of the Siamese Schools (Sukhothai), and of the half-closed eyes that seem to prepare for the transition between the eyes of the Angkor Vat style, which are generally open, and the closed eyes of the Bàyon style. But recent discoveries have demonstrated that Khmer art had produced a long line of Buddhas sheltered by the Nāga, such as the one in Figure XVI, where nothing had been borrowed from outside arts. Also, the physical type and the conventions which appear in this work did not assert themselves until quite late. Had the Buddhas of the "Commaille" type continued to be dated to an earlier period than the works characteristic of the Bàyon style, they would be marking a break of sorts within a family whose continuity now seems well established. Nothing justifies this: the transition between open eyes and eyes that are closed indicates a conceptual change which does not necessarily involve an evolution through a phase when the eyelids are lowered. Meditation is translated by closed eyes (Figure IX), and it is only natural to extend the scheme to Buddhist images, since it is the meditation of the Master that gives birth to the possibility of salvation for his followers.

It also seems that within a problem which happens to be a very complex one, the reflection of Siamese traits that we notice in the "Commaille" Buddha indicates the time when foreign influence began to make itself felt in a more pronounced way. This influence led Khmer statuary to its later forms where Khmer and Thai aesthetics balanced each other in a harmonious compromise. We are consequently inclined to suggest for images of this family a date close to the middle of the XIIIth century, at the earliest, and in any case postdating the reign of Jayavarman VII. They could represent the production of the Theravāda schools which were probably launched during that reign, but only asserted themselves little by little, with the advance of the new Faith.

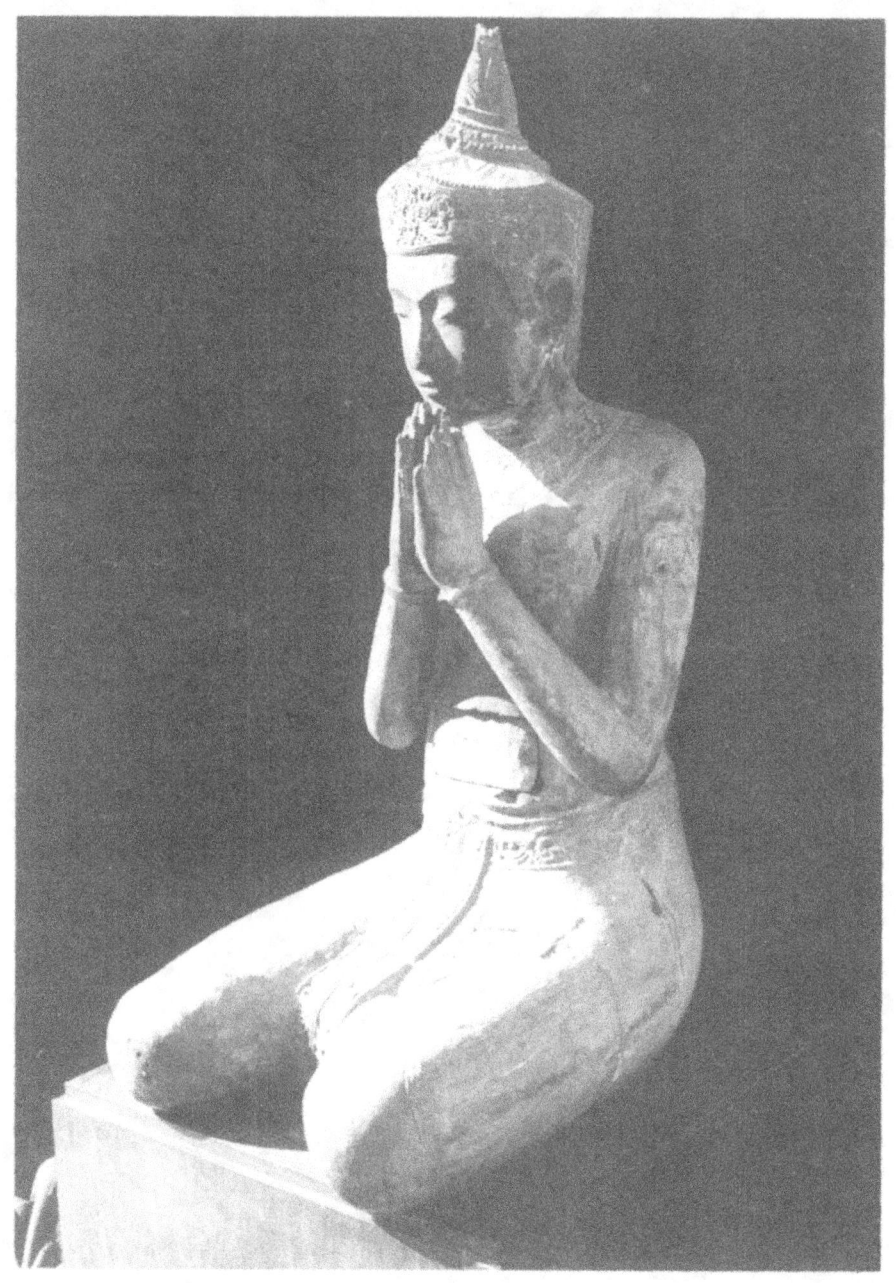

FIGURE XXIV

FIGURE XXIV

Orant (Kneeling figure) (J-11, 4)

Wood (H. 0 m. 92—36 7/32"), Angkor Vat
Approximately XVth century

It is customary to limit the study of Khmer statuary to works of the XIIIth century. This unfavorable prejudice weighs heavily on later works which are all grouped together, and regarded as products of a lesser art. While it is true that the constant, almost mechanical recurrence of the same types denotes a relative mediocrity, that Thai influence becomes increasingly evident and imposes its clichés, the fact remains that some of the works are very worthy of interest.[1]

But it must also be said that in time stone statues became much rarer and tended to be replaced by wood sculptures made from choice, almost indestructible materials. The change, which may derive from an attempt to ease the task, was no doubt mainly due to the scarcity of good quality sandstone that had already made itself felt back in the Bàyon period, and to the increase of commissions which resulted from the progress of the new Faith. Late stone statues were nearly always made with very poor quality sandstone, with no resistance, which flake rapidly. Even when their dimensions did not exceed human size, the statues were occasionally assembled with small blocks.

The art that asserted itself with Theravāda Buddhism (often designated as Hīnayānist), used stone only rarely; lacquering and coating protected the polychromed statues, but only traces of the pigment have survived in this one.

This figure, kneeling in an attitude of humility, remains very Khmer in spirit. The forms, and even the features have not been, so to speak, "contaminated." The *sarong* is not very visible, but its shape is still Khmer. The vertical decorated band had appeared in Buddhist bas-reliefs back at the end of the XIIth century. This one, however, is an already poorly understood recollection because the belt that should normally hold everything in place, slides underneath this strip of cloth which has now acquired a purely decorative significance. The adornment, on the contrary, is clearly Thai: the high necklace, the belt, and the diadem in particular are in contrast with the Khmer compositions of the Angkorean period. The decoration of the adornment had always included geometric elements that have now disappeared, giving way to floral foliate motifs. But this transformation is only superficial, and the feeling of humble piety, the contemplative character, and the gentleness of the work denote an art still very lively, and strongly traditional.

---

[1]M. Giteau, "Iconographie du Cambodge post-angkorien" (*Publications de l'Ecole française d'Extrême-Orient*, Paris 1975).

GLOSSARY

Abhayamudrā (Skt.)[*] – Gesture of dispelling fear.

Airavāta (Skt.) – Three-headed elephant, Indra's vehicle.

Akshobya (Skt.) – "Imperturbable." In Mahāyāna, the transcendental Buddha of the Eastern region of the Universe. He performs the *bhūmisparśamudrā*, the "Earth touching" gesture.

Amitābha (Skt.) – "Infinite Light." In Mahāyāna, the transcendental Buddha of the Western region of the Universe. He is shown seated in meditation.

Amoghasiddhi (Skt.) – "Infallible Success." In Mahāyāna, the transcendental Buddha of the Northern region of the Universe. He performs the *abhayamudrā*, the gesture of dispelling fear.

Ananta (Skt.) – cf. Śesa.

Angkor (Kh.) – From Skt. "Nagara," town, city. The royal city, the capital.

Angkor Thom (Kh.) – The "great," the "grand," city built by Jayavarman VII [1181–ca. 1219 (?)], centered on the Bàyon.

Antaravāsaka (Skt., P.) – Undergarment covering the lower part of the body of the Buddha or of a Buddhist monk.

Apsaras (Skt.) – A feminine deity, or semi-divine.

Asura (Skt.) – Generally a demon, endowed with power similar to that of gods.

Avalokiteśvara (Skt.) – The "Compassionate," the "Lord who looks down (with compassion)"; one of the most popular Bodhisattvas of the Mahāyāna, he bears an image of Amithāba in his headdress. He can assume many different aspects; in his "radiant" aspect his body is covered with a multitude of tiny Buddha images. A very important figure in Khmer iconography of the Bàyon style. Lokeśvara (Skt.) – "Lord of the World" is one of the most usual names of Avalokiteśvara.

Avatāra (Skt.) – Descent; in particular incarnation of a deity on earth, especially that of Vishnu for the salvation of beings. For the list of Vishnu's ten major *avatāra*, cf. Nota at the end of the Glossary. For the list of Vishnu's usual attributes, cf. Vishnu.

Balarāma (Skt.) – Older "twin" brother of Krishna; Vishnu's 8th major *avatāra*.

---

[*] Engl., English; Fr., French; Kh., Khmer; P., Pāli; Skt., Sanskrit; Th., Thai; m., masculine; f., feminine.

Banteay / Banteai (Kh.) – Citadel, name given to temples having an important enclosing wall.

Bàray / Bàrai (Kh.) – Man-controlled large body of water.

Beng (Kh.) – Pond.

Bhūmisparśamudrā (Skt.) – Gesture of the Buddha calling the Earth to witness, representing his victory over Māra.

Bodhi (Skt., P.) – Perfect Knowledge and Supreme Enlightenment which results in Buddhahood.

Bodhimanda (Skt.) – The site, the seat of the Enlightenment at Bodh Gayā (Mahābodhi). The sacred spot where all the successive Buddhas have attained or will attain Full Enlightenment. (cf. Sambodhi).

Bodhisattva (Skt.), Bodhisatta (P.) – Meaning "Intended for Enlightenment." In Theravāda Buddhism, a being who has reached the state preceding the final liberation. In Mahāyāna, one who postpones his own Nirvāna for the sake of helping other beings.

Brahmā (Skt., P.) – One of the principal three gods of Hinduism. Creator of the Universe, dispensor of the *Veda*. Four-faced, four-armed divinity born of the golden lotus that grew from Vishnu's navel when he awoke from his cosmic sleep.

Brāhmanism—The early religion of India issued from Vedism. A cult based on the authority of the Priests (Brahmins), later confused with Hinduism.

Buddha (Skt., P.) – "Enlightened One," as Śākyamuni the historical Buddha of our times. One of a number of the Buddhas of the Past whose careers were the same as that of the historical Buddha. The transcendental Buddhas or Dhyāni-Buddhas are peculiar to the Mahāyāna. In Hinduism the historical Buddha is considered to be the 9th major *avatāra* of Vishnu manifested in our time.

Buddhapāda (Skt., P.) – The Buddha's footprint.

Cakra (Skt.) – Wheel, solar disc; disc-like weapon attribute of Vishnu, usually carried in his upper right hand. In Buddhism, surrounded by 2 gazelles it is the symbol of the Doctrine and of the Buddha's First Sermon in the Deer Park at Sarnath where the Wheel, (i.e., the Buddhist Law) was set in motion.

Cakravartin (Skt.) – Universal Monarch, world ruler or "Sovereign of the Wheel."

Champa – An ancient Indianized kingdom situated on the East and Southeast coast of the Indochinese peninsula, today the central part of Viêt Nam.

Conch (Engl.), Śaṅkha (Skt.) – A spiral one-piece shell; attribute of Vishnu usually carried in his upper left hand.

Deva, Devatā (Skt., P.) – God, deity of undetermined rank living on earth or on heavenly levels.

Devarāja (Skt.) – God-king. Name of the Supreme God in the ritual instituted by Jayavarman II on Mt. Mahendra (present-day Phnom Kulên).

Devī (Skt.) – The Great Goddess. Personified feminine energy (*śakti*) of Śiva assuming his various kind or terrifying aspects.

Dharma (Skt.) – The Law which rules the true order of affairs and the relation between beings and things. In Buddhist usage the teaching of the Buddha, conceived as the final and absolute truth.

Dharmacakra (Skt.) – The Wheel of the Law. In Buddhism, it symbolizes the Buddhist Doctrine.

Dharmacakramudrā (Skt.) – Gesture of setting in motion the Wheel of the Law symbolizing the First Sermon the Buddha preached in the Deer Park at Sarnath. Also known as the *dharmacakra-pravartana-mudrā*. This gesture was not used in Khmer iconography.

Dharmaśālā (Skt.) – Shelter for pilgrims and travelers.

Dhoti (Hindi) – A male garment consisting of a piece of cloth wrapped around the waist and ending above the knees or at the ankles.

Dhyānamudrā (Skt.) – cf. Samādhi.

Dhyāni-Buddhas, from Dhyāna (Skt.): meditation. The transcendental Buddhas of the Mahāyāna, the Meditating Buddhas, also known as Contemplative Buddhas. They are five, cf. Vairocana, Akshobhya, Ratnasambhava, Amitābha, Amoghasiddhi.

Dikpāla (Skt.) – Guardian of one of the four cardinal points. Also Lokapāla.

Dīpaṅkara (Skt.) – Name of the Buddha of the Past, first of the 24 Predecessors of the Buddha of our time.

Durgā (Skt.) – The fierce aspect of Devī; the "Unconquerable"; the Great Goddess slayer of the demonical Buffalo Mahishā, also known as Mahishāsuramardinī.

Dvārapāla (Skt.) – Door or gate guardian.

Enlightenment – cf. Bodhimanda.

Funan – Name given by the Chinese to the ancient Indianized kingdom in the Indo-chinese Peninsula, in the lower Mekong basin, founded about the Ist century AD, and well established in the Vth century. In the VIth century it was taken over by Zhenla, a former vassal state, thus giving rise to the Khmer empire.

Gana (Skt., P.) – Group of attendants of Śiva, kind of dwarfs endowed with an animal head. They reside on the slopes of Mt. Kailāsa, Śiva's residence.

Gandharva (Skt.) – A class of semi-divine heavenly musicians.

Ganeśa (Skt.) – "Lord of the Gana." Son of Pārvatī and Śiva. God of knowledge and intelligence, destroyer of obstacles. Represented as an obese human figure with the head of an elephant.

Garuda (Skt.) – Mythical bird, king of the birds and natural enemy of the snakes; Vishnu's vehicle. In Khmer art, usually represented with human arms and a rather human torso; he has a beak, wings, legs, and claws of an eagle.

Gautama (Skt.), Gotama (P.) – Name of the historical Buddha, after the name of the paternal clan. Descendant of the Brahmanic ascetic Gautama.

Gopura (Skt.) – Entrance pavilion to various precincts of temples and to cities.

Great Departure – The decisive moment in the career of the historical Buddha when, on the night of his 29th birthday, renouncing his princely life, all worldly possessions and attachments, he left his family and palace with the assistance of the gods in order to become a mendicant monk and devote himself to meditation.

Guru (Skt.) – Spiritual teacher.

Hamsa (Skt.) – Sacred goose residing in the Himalayas. The vehicle of Brahmā and occasionally of Varuna, the god ruling the West.

Hanchement (Fr.) – A more or less pronounced sway-hip stance where one hip is generally lower than the other.

Hanumān (Skt.) – Semi-divine monkey, chief of the army of monkeys in the Rāmāyana; ally of Rāma.

Harihara (Skt.) – Brahmanic divinity who combines the names and the features of Vishnu (Hari) and Śiva (Hara). It represents the merger of the two divinities into one, endowed with the attributes of both gods.

Hevajra (Skt.) – Also called Heruka. Divinity of Tantric Mahāyāna, fierce manifestation of the transcendental Buddha Akshobya. In iconography often shown with 8 heads, 16 arms, and 4 feet, dancing on a demon.

Hīnayāna (Skt.) – "Inferior way," "Minor Vehicle," "Lesser Means of Progression." Name used pejoratively by Mahāyāna Buddhists when referring to the non-Mahāyāna sects which adhere strictly to early Buddhist traditions.

Hinduism – Any of the various forms of Brāhmanism later modified with additions of philosophical ideas. The religion and social system of the Hindus.

Indra (Skt.), **Inda** (P.) – Vedic god, sovereign of the Heaven of the 33 gods [Trayastrimśa (Skt.), Tāvatimsa (P.)], dwelling on the summit of Mt. Meru. His personal name is Śakra (Skt.) or Sakka (P.). Name mostly used in Buddhism where he is a devotee of the Buddha. His attribute is the thunderbolt.

Iśvara (Skt.) – The Lord, one of the names for Śiva.

Jatā (Skt., P.) – Braided chignon worn by ascetics and Śiva; also *jatāmukuta* – chignon, crown of hair.

Jātaka (Skt., P.) – "Birth"; stories of the previous births of the Buddha Gautama illustrating his progress as an animal or human toward Buddhahood. Each of the 550 *Jātaka* is designated by the name of the hero of the story.

Jina (Skt., P.) – The "Conqueror." In Buddhism the term designates the historical Buddha as well as, and especially, the transcendental Buddhas of the Mahāyāna.

Kailāsa (Skt.) – Name of the mountain, Śiva's residence in the Himalayas.

Kāla (Skt., P.) – "Time," "Death"; the destructor of time, destiny, death. One of the names for Yama, the god of the dead.

Kālī (Skt.) – Black, terrifying manifestation of Devī.

Kalpa (Skt.), **Kappa** (P.) – A day of Brahmā, equal to 4,320 million years of mortals, duration of a cosmic period.

Kalkyāvatāra or Kalkin (Skt.) – The 10th major *avatāra* of Vishnu, still not manifested; represented as a knight riding a horse or as a horse.

Kambuja (Skt.) – Name of the Khmers supposedly descendents of Kambu Svāyambhuva, their eponymous ancestor. The name is preserved in "Cambodia" and "Kambuchea" or "Kampuchea."

Kapilavastu (Skt.), Kapilavatthu (P.) – cf. Śākya.

Kārtikkeya – cf. Skanda.

Kinnara (m.), Kinnari (f.) (Skt., P.) – Mythical Himalayan figures, part human and part horse or mostly with the head of a bird, or a human bust. Often represented as flying musicians.

Kīrtimukha (Skt.) – "Face of Glory." A creature issued from Śiva's anger. Bid by him to devour its own body it was left with a leontine head only. With arms and sometimes with horns, it is shown spitting forth scrolls of foliage. A symbol of prosperity, occasionally mistaken for Simhamukha and for the mask of Kāla.

Kô (Kh.) – Bullock.

Kompong (Kh.) – Wharf.

Krishna (Skt.) – The "Dark one." One whose complexion is dark. The 8th major, and one of the most popular incarnations of Vishnu.

Kūrma (Skt.) – Tortoise with a human torso. Vishnu's 2nd major *avatāra.*

Kuvera (Skt., P.) – The god of wealth, regent of the North. Best known in Buddhism under his patronym Vaisravana (Skt.) or Vessanava (P.). Often represented as an obese figure carrying a purse and accompanied by the Seven Treasures.

Lakshana (Skt.), Lakkhana (P.) – Mark, sign, auspicious attribute. Marks of the "Great Man": the 32 major marks described in the Buddhist scriptures which are the physical characteristics that bear witness to the accrual of merits in previous lives whereby the predestination of the Cakravartin and of the Buddha may be recognized at birth.

Lakshmana (Skt.) – Rāma's younger brother, and his companion in the Rāmāyana epic.

Lakshmī (Skt.) – Brahmanic divinity. Goddess of good fortune, prosperity, and beauty. Vishnu's *śakti* or feminine energy. Mother of Kāma, the god of love; also known as Srī. She is generally believed to be born of the Churning of the Ocean. Her emblem is the lotus. cf. Srī.

Lalitāsana (Skt.) – Seated attitude with the right leg folded and the left leg hanging down.

Liṅga (Skt.) – Emblem, phallus. Symbolic representation of Śiva as a stylized phallus. Of different types and made of different materials, *liṅga* are often divided into 3 parts: the cubic part represents Brahmā, the octagonal prism represents Vishnu and the cylindrical section with a rounded top represents Śiva. cf. *mukhaliṅga.*

Lokeśvara (Skt.) – cf. Avalokiteśvara.

Mahābhārata (Skt.) – The Great Indian epic, the "Great discourse" of more than 90,000 verses written in Sanskrit, narrating the rivalry between the Pāndava and the Kaurava.

Mahābodhi (Skt., P.) – Name of the Tree of Enlightenment, and more generally of the sanctuary erected at Bodh Gaya on the site of the Buddha's Enlightenment, cf. Bodhimanda.

Mahādeva (Skt.) – The Great god, i.e., Śiva.

Mahāparinirvāna (Skt.), Mahāparinibbana (P.) – The Great Total Extinction of the Buddha at Kuśinagara which occurred after he had assembled all the faithful for his final sermon.

Mahāpurusha (Skt.), Mahāpurisa (P.) – Great or Eminent man; ascetic, sage. In Buddhism, one endowed with the *lakshana* and destined to become a Universal Monarch or a Buddha.

Mahāyāna (Skt.) – The "Great Vehicle" or "Greater Means of Progression." Advanced doctrine derived from early Buddhism. In giving an essential role to Bodhisattvas and the transfer of their merits it is considered to lead more efficiently to salvation.

Mahendraparvata (Skt.) – One of the seven chains of mountains of the Himalaya. In Cambodia, the early name for Phnom Kulên. By setting up the Royal Liṅga there and initiating the Devarāja cult Jayavarman II (802-850), was consecrated Universal Monarch of his kingdom and declared it secure from Java, thus giving rise to the Angkorian Monarchy.

Maheśvara (Skt.) – The Great Lord Śiva.

Maitreya (Skt.), Metteya (P.) – The "Benevolent," Bodhisattva residing in the Tushita Heaven, he will be the Buddha of future times. One of the great Bodhisattvas of Mahāyāna, his emblem is a small *stūpa* in his headdress.

Makara (Skt., P.) – Mythical aquatic animal combining the characteristics of a crocodile and of a dolphin, and having a trunk. Sometimes ridden by Varuna, the god ruling the West. An architectural decoration, mostly associated with Kīrtimukha or Kāla.

Mandala (Skt., P.) – Circle, disc, or circular arrangement. A sacrificial area; a magic chart divided geometrically with representations of divinities or of Buddhas and their pantheons.

Māra (Skt., P.) – The forces of Evil. One of the most powerful gods in the Realm of Desires and Death, insofar as his masterful attempts to thwart the Enlightenment of the Buddha and his teaching. Considered to be the Temptor, the Cunning one.

Māravijaya (Skt., P.) – "Victory over Māra." Epithet given to the Buddha after his triumph over the army of demons Māra sent against him, compelling the Evil god to recognize his pre-eminence. The event is symbolized by the *bhūmisparśa-mudrā*, the gesture of calling the Earth to witness.

Matsya (Skt.) – Fish with a human torso. Vishnu's first major *avatāra*.

Men (Kh., Th.) – Khmer and Thai pronunciation of Meru. Light pavilion used for cremation.

Meru (Skt., P.) – Name of the mythical mountain (also often called Sineru in Buddhist Scriptures), axis of the world around which the continents and the oceans are ordered. At its summit is the abode of the Trayastrimśa (the 33 gods), with Indra as its sovereign.

Mucilinda (Skt.), Mucalinda (P.) – Serpentine semi-divine being, a *nāga* king who, during the 6th week after the attainment of Enlightenment, protected the meditation of the Buddha from the torrential rains and the cold by surrounding him with the coils of his body and his spread-out multi-headed hood.

Mudrā (Skt.) – Mark, seal; gesture of the hand and fingers having symbolic significance. In Mahāyāna, referring to the Buddha and especially to the transcendantal Buddhas.

Mukhaliṅga (Skt.) – Face *liṅga*, a *liṅga* bearing one (*ekamukhaliṅga*), or four (*caturmukhaliṅga*), or five (*pañcamukhaliṅga*) faces of Śiva engraved or rendered in high relief.

Mukuta / Makuta (Skt., P.) – A patterned headdress fitting over the head.

Nāga (m.), Nāgī (f.) (Skt., P.) – Mythical, hybrid, semi-divine beings, part-snake part-human, with the power to assume the shape of either one. *Nāga* dwell in the subterranean and watery regions, guard the treasures, and are endowed with a very long life. Some *nāga* are pious devotees of the Buddha.

Nāgarāja (Skt.) – King of the *Nāga*.

Nandin (Skt.) – "Joy"; name of the white bull, vehicle of Śiva and his companion. An image of Nandin appears in all Śivaite temples facing the sanctuary of the god.

Nandīśa or Nandikeśvara (Skt.) – Name of the chief of Gana, principal assistant of Śiva, and door-keeper with Mahākāla.

Narasimha (Skt.) – "Man-lion"; Vishnu's 4th major *avatāra* with the head of a lion and the body of a man.

Nirvāna (Skt.), Nibbāna (P.) – The "Extinction" and final liberation from the cycle of rebirths.

Padmapāni (Skt.) – "Lotus in hand." Epithet and name of Avalokiteśvara and in particular, non-Tantric aspect of the divinity.

Padmāsana (Skt.) – Lotus seat in the form of a lotus in full bloom with the seat at its center. Also term used to define the attitude of a deity seated in *vajrāsana*.

Pagoda – Generally speaking a Buddhist monastery, especially for Cambodia, Laos, and Viêt Nam, or *stūpa*, particularly for Burma and China. This word is of Portuguese origin.

Pāli – Language of ancient India. The early-middle Indian dialect used by Theravāda Buddhism in Sri Lanka and the Indochinese Peninsula.

Paraśurāma (Skt.) – "Rāma with the axe." Vishnu's 6th major *avatāra*.

Paridhāna (Skt.) – Garment, a rectangular piece of cloth tied around the waist that can be draped in different ways, but always covering the legs.

Pārvatī (Skt.) – "Daughter of the Mountain." One of the names for, and kind aspect of Devī, the Goddess, Śiva's *śakti*.

Phnom (Kh.) – Mountain, hill; also used traditionally to designate a temple, a sanctuary, or a sacred site.

Pradakshinā (Skt.) – Ritual circumambulation always leaving the monument on the right, i.e, clockwise.

Prah (Kh.) – Holy, sacred.

Prajñāpāramitā (Skt.) – "Perfection of Wisdom." In Mahāyāna, feminine form of Bodhisattva sometimes presented as the spiritual Mother of all the Buddhas; philosophical aspect of Tārā. She carries the book (of knowledge).

Prasat (Kh.) from Prāsāda (Skt.) – Palace, Temple. In Cambodia generally designating the tower, the shrine itself.

Prasāvya (Skt.) – Ritual circumambulation having a funerary character, and always leaving the monument on the left, i.e. counter-clockwise.

Prey / Prei (Kh.) – Forest.

Purāna (Skt.) – Archaic text, historical legend of India.

Rākshasa (Skt.), Rakkhasa (P.) – Type of nocturnal demons usually malevolent, that one should guard against. They are at times considered to be *yaksha*, at others as *asura* or demons.

Rāma (Skt.) – Vishnu's 7th major *avatāra* prompted by the request of the gods to be delivered from the demons (*Rākshasa*). The hero of the Rāmāyana.

Rāmāyana (Skt.) – The epic poem attributed to Vālmīki, presumably written before 100 B.C., narrating the story of Rāma, his birth, the abduction of his wife Sītā by Rāvana, the lord of the demons reigning at Laṅkā, and his victorious war against him. It became known throughout Southeast Asia as "The glory of Rāma." (Th. Ramakien , Kh. Reamker).

Ratnasambhava (Skt.) – "Jewel-born." In Mahāyāna, the transcendental Buddha of the Southern region of the Universe. He performs the *varadamudrā*, the gesture of charity.

Rāvana (Skt.) – "The Lord of the Rākshasa," half-brother of Kuvera, sovereign of Laṅkā. His abduction of Sītā and battle against Rāma are the esssential parts of the Rāmāyana. He is depicted with 10 heads and 20 arms.

Rishi (Skt.), Issi (P.) – Sage, ascetic, hermit. Holy personage who received the revelation of Vedic Hymns. The Himalayas are the favorite abode of the *rishi*.

Sadāśiva (Skt.) – The "ever benevolent" Śiva. The supreme aspect of Śiva. Usually shown with 5 heads and 10 arms.

Śakra (Skt.), Sakka (P.) – cf. Indra.

Śakti (Skt.) – Energy; the active power of a deity represented in the feminine form and regarded as the consort of the god.

Śākya (Skt.), Sakyā, Sākiya (P.) – Clan residing in Kapilavastu (a section of the Himalayan region that roughly corresponds to the south of present-day Nepal), into which was born Prince Siddhārtha the last incarnation of the Buddha. Śākyamuni, the "Sage of the Śākya" was one name for the historical Buddha.

Samādhi (Skt.) – The attitude of meditation; seated cross-legged in the Indian fashion, both hands resting on each other in the lap (the gesture of the hands is also called *dhyānamudrā,* and has roughly the same meaning). In Mahāyāna, the characteristic posture of Amitābha.

Sambodhi (Skt., P.) – "Full Enlightenment." Supreme attainment characteristic of the Buddha.

Samghāti (Skt., P.) – One of the three garments of a Buddhist monk; a shawl of sorts that can be worn over the *uttarāsaṅga.* Rarely worn in Southeast Asia except for some ceremonial occasions when it is folded over the left shoulder.

Sampot (Kh.) – Cambodian or Thai garment, a piece of rectangular cloth worn around the hips and tied in front; the edges of the cloth are inserted between the legs and fastened in the back of the belt.

Sanskrit – An Indo-European language; in its earliest form it dates from the Vedic period. The sacred language of Hinduism, also used in Buddhism, especially in Mahāyāna and Hīnayāna.

Sarasvatī (Skt.) – Goddess of speech. Brahmā's consort.

Śesha (Skt.) – Name of the mythical snake "with a thousand heads" upon which Vishnu rests during the night that separates two cosmic periods. Also known as Ananta "The Infinite."

Siddhārtha (Skt.) – i.e., "goal reached." cf. Śākya.

Simhamukha (Skt.) – Leonine face or mask. Head of a monster seen in Indian and Khmer art, and occasionally the vehicle of some divinity. Often called Kīrtimukha or Kāla.

Sītā (Skt.) – "Furrow." The wife of Rāma, born from a furrow (in the earth). Abducted by Rāvana in the Rāmāyana.

Śiva (Skt.) – One of the three principal gods of Hinduism corresponding to the Vedic divinity Rudra; master of the *yogi* and supreme god of various Śivaite sects. In Buddhism he is inferior to the Trayastrimśa (the 33 gods), but is considered to be the most powerful god on earth.

Skanda (Skt) – A Brahmanic divinity, the god of war, also known as Kārttikeya. Son of Śiva, forever youthful, he wears his hair in the 3 or 5 locks of adolescent boys. His vehicle is the peacock.

Śrī (Skt.) – Fortune, prosperity, beauty; name of Lakshmī. Also honorary title for divinities and sovereigns.

Stŭng (Kh.) – River.

Stūpa (Skt.), Thūpa (P.) – Originally meaning tumulus or burial mound. It very early became the most important type of Buddhist monument and was gradually enhanced with a very elaborate symbolism. Essentially, a *stūpa* is a reliquary or a commemorative monument consisting of a dome supported by a base and surmounted by tiered parasols.

Sugrīva (Skt.) – The king of monkeys deposed by his brother Valīn; reinstated by Rāma and his ally in the Rāmāyana.

Sujātā (Skt., P.) – Name of a pious woman from whom the future Buddha accepted the offering of food, thus putting an end to the long and exhausting austerities to which he had subjected himself.

Sūrya (Skt.), Sūriya (P.) – The Brahmanic Sun-god represented with a lotus in each hand. He rides a chariot generally drawn by 7 horses.

Tantra (Skt.) – Doctrine, rule, theory and especially the esoteric doctrines that make much use of magic formulas. Arising on the Indian sub-continent as a movement in the VIth century, the ritualistic practices of Tantrism penetrated both the late Mahāyāna and Brahmanic cults.

Tārā (Skt.) – The "Saviouress," "Who enables to cross over." In Mahāyāna, a sort of feminine Bodhisattva, assistant or companion of Avalokiteśvara. In Tantrism she can form a couple with the transcendental Buddhas.

Theravāda (P.) – "Doctrine of the Elders" representing the traditional Pāli heritage of early Buddhism. The Pāli canon is considered by the Theravāda sects to be the authentic doctrine. Stavīravāda (Skt.).

Thom (Kh.) – Large, big, great.

Trayastrimśa (Skt.), Tāvatimsa (P.) – The 33 gods governed by Indra, dwelling on Mt. Meru, who keep the world in proper working order. The Buddha went up to the Heaven of the 33 to teach the Law to his mother, reborn in the Tushita Heaven, who came down to the Heaven of the 33 in order to hear him.

Tribhaṅga (Skt.) – Triple flexion; the attitude with a pronounced sway of the hip characteristic of Indian statuary where the shoulder line and the hip line follow nearly parallel directions.

Trimūrti (Skt.) – Brahmanic divine trinity made up of Śiva, Vishnu, and Brahmā.

Triśūla (Skt.) – Trident, weapon attribute of Śiva and also sometimes his symbol.

Trivikrama (Skt.) – "Three strides." The function and aspect of Vāmana the dwarf Brahman, Vishnu's 5th major *avatāra* when he conquered the Three Worlds in three strides over the demon Bali, but left him the underworld.

Tushita (Skt.), Tusita (P.) – One of the heavens in the Realm of Desires, way above Mt. Meru, where dwell the gods in aerial palaces, the Bodhisattvas awaiting their final existence on earth, and the deceased mothers of all the Buddhas.

Umā (Skt.) – "Light." One of the names for, and kind aspect of Devī, Śiva's *śakti*.

Ūrnā (Skt.), Unnā (P.) – Tuft of hair between the eyebrows of the Buddha; one of the Lakshana. The *ūrnā* is rarely indicated in the art of Cambodia, Thailand, and Laos.

Ushnīsha (Skt.), Unhīsa (P.) – Topknot, cranial protuberance of the Buddha; one of the *lakshana*.

Uttarāsanga (Skt., P.) – The robe, the outer garment worn by the Buddha or a Buddhist monk.

Vāhana (Skt.) – Mount, vehicle, especially of a deity.

Vairocana (Skt.) – "Resplendent." In Mahāyāna, the transcendental Buddha of the zenith of the Universe. Represented making the "preaching" gesture (*dharmacakramudrā*).

Vājimukha (Skt.) – "Face of Horse." In Hinduism, a divinity with the head of a horse. A minor *avatāra* of Vishnu.

Vajra (Skt.), Vajira (P.) – Thunder, diamond. Indra's and Vajrapāni's weapon, the thunderbolt. In later Buddhism characteristic of the Vajrayāna, a form of Tantric Buddhism, the means of progression through the Diamond, the "Diamond Vehicle."

Vajradhara (Skt.) – "Thunder bearer." A name which can designate the transcendental Buddha Vajrasattva, pre-eminent in the group of *Jina*, the Bodhisattva Vajrapāni or one of the 16 Vajra-Bodhisattvas of Tantric Mahāyāna.

Vajrapāni (Skt.) – "Thunder in hand." In early forms of esoteric Buddhism, name of a *yaksha* assigned to the person and the service of the Buddha, same as Indra. In Mahāyāna, Bodhisattva assistant of the Buddha more or less associated with Avalokiteśvara.

Vajrāsana (Skt.) – Adamantine posture. Seated attitude with legs crossed and each foot resting on the opposite thigh, the soles turned upward (also called *vajraparyanka* or *padmāsana*). Attitude unknown in Khmer iconography.

Vajrasattva (Skt.) – Buddha of the late Mahāyāna (sometimes also a Bodhisattva); the "being with a thunderbolt."

Varadamudrā (Skt.) – Gesture of bestowing favors or charity. Gesture of giving and receiving. The right hand (usually) is open and the hand is extended. In Mahāyāna the gesture of the transcendental Buddha Ratnasambhava.

Varāha (Skt.) – Man with the head of a boar; Vishnu's 3rd major *avatāra*.

. . . varman (Kh.) – "Protected by," "who has . . . for cuirass." Title assumed by various lines of sovereigns and especially by Khmer kings.

Vāsuki (Skt.) – The serpent king used as a cord in the Churning of the Ocean.

Vat Phu (Kh.) – The archaeological site of ancient Zhenla situated at the foot of the mountain called Lingaparvata in Khmer inscriptions, located in the proximity of the Mekong in the southeast of present-day Laos. The group of monuments was Śivaite at first, and later Buddhist. Sacred spot of the Kambujas.

Vat or Wat (Kh., Th.) – A group of structures that constitute a Buddhist monastery in Cambodia, Thailand, Laos; generally translated as Temple.

Veda (Skt.) – Sacred knowledge, revelation. Originally a verbal tradition; it is the most sacred Hindu book made up of four *Veda*, the earliest and the most sacred one being the *Rig Veda* which goes back to ca. 1200 BC.

Vihāra (Skt.) – Originally the dwelling place of the monks, it came to house Buddhist images. It often occupied the center of a courtyard surrounded by a cloister where additional statues of the Buddha are erected.

Vīrāsana (Skt.) – "The seat of the hero." The seated attitude where the legs are folded, one lying on top of the other; usually the right leg lies on the left leg. Attitude in keeping with the iconography of South India, Sri Lanka, Cambodia, Champa, Thailand.

Vishnu (Skt.) – One of the three principal gods of Hinduism. Benevolent, Keeper and Saviour of the world, and protector of humans. Usually represented with 4 arms, he can be designated by 1,000 names corresponding to his various shapes and activities. He reveals himself in 10 major incarnations or descents (*avatāra*) in order to save the world. For his 10 major *avatāra*, cf. Nota. The usual attributes of Vishnu are:

> The conch (*śankha*, Skt.)
> The disc (*cakra*, Skt.)
> The club (*gadā*, Skt.)
> The pink lotus (*padma*, Skt.)

In Khmer and Cham iconography, as well as in that of Dvāravatī, the lotus is replaced by the Earth (Dharani, Skt.)

Viśvakarman (Skt.), **Vissukamma** (P.) – God of the Heaven of the Thirty-three. Celestial architect of the gods.

Vitarkamudrā (Skt.) – Gesture of argumentation (exposition). The hand or both hands are half-open, the thumb and usually the index finger are joined. In South India, Cambodia, Thailand, Laos, and Champa it is substituted for the *dharmacakramudrā*.

Yaksha (m.), **Yakshinī** (f.) (Skt.), **Yakkha** (m.), **Yakkhinī** (f.) (P.) – Mythical and supernatural beings. They may be kind or menacing, some are cannibalistic. Some attend the gods, others, having received the teaching of the Buddha became his zealots. As local divinities or tree spirits they can be worshiped in their own rights.

Yama (Skt., P.) – God of the dead, judge of the dead, regent of the South quarter.

Yoga (Skt., P.) – A system of physical and spiritual discipline designated to give mastery over body and mind. Originating in ancient times these excercises were, and are used in Buddhism and in Hinduism. The *yogi* master the *yoga*. The ascetics practice *yoga*.

Zhenla – Name given by the Chinese to the ancient Indianized state originally located south of present-day Laos in the region of Vat Phu, and towards the junction of the middle course of the Mae Nam and of the river Mun. At first Zhenla was a vassal state of Funan which it conquered in mid-VIth century. The Khmer kings considered Zhenla as the true cradle of their civilization.

NOTA. The 10 major *avatāra* of Vishnu:

1. Matsya, or fish with a human torso
2. Kūrma, or tortoise with a human torso
3. Varāha, or man with the head of a boar
4. Narasimha, or "man-lion"
5. Vāmana, or human dwarf
6. Paraśurāma, or Rāma with the axe, human form
7. Rāma, human form, hero of the Rāmāyana
8. Balarāma and Krishna, the two brothers, human form
9. The Buddha, human form
10. Kalkin, knight riding a horse, or horse

Selected Bibliography

I. GENERAL WORKS

J. Boisselier. *Il Sud-Est Asiatico* (Storia Universale dell'Arte, Torino, 1986).

G. Cœdès. *Les Peuples de la Péninsule indochinoise* (Paris 1962).

——. *Indianized States of Southeast Asia* (Honolulu, 1968).

L. Fréderic. *The Art of Southeast Asia* (Abrams, New York).

M. Giteau. *The Civilization of Angkor* (New York, 1976).

B.-Ph. Groslier. *Indochina* (Archaeologia Mundi, Geneva, 1966).

G. Groslier. *Recherches sur les Cambodgiens* (Paris, 1921).

G. Porée, E. Maspero. *Mœurs et coutumes des Khmers* (Paris, 1938).

S. Thierry. *Les Khmers* (Paris, 1964).

II. HISTORY, EPIGRAPHY

A. Barth. *Inscriptions sanscrites du Cambodge* (Paris, 1885).

A. Bergaigne. *Inscriptions sanscrites du Cambodge et de Campā* (Paris, 1893).

L. P. Briggs. *The Ancient Khmer Empire* (Philadelphia, 1951).

G. Cœdès. *Inscriptions du Cambodge*, t. I–VIII (E.F.E.O., 1937–1966).

M. Giteau. *Histoire du Cambodge* (Paris, 1957).

Tchéou Ta-Kouan. *Mémoires sur les coutumes du Cambodge* (traduction P. Pelliot). (N^lle^ édition, Paris 1951).

III. RELIGIONS

K. Bhattacharya. *Les religions brahmaniques dans l'ancien Cambodge* (Publications E.F.E.O., 1961).

G. Cœdès. *Angkor, an Introduction* (translated by Emily Floyd Gardiner, Hong Kong, 1963).

L. Malleret. *Pour comprendre la sculpture buddhique et brahmanique en Indochine* (Saigon, 1942).

IV. ART AND ARCHAEOLOGY

M. Bénisti. *Rapports entre le premier art khmer et l'art indien* (Publications E.F.E.O., 1970).

J. Boisselier. *La statuaire khmère et son évolution* (Publications E.F.E.O., 1955).

——. *Le Cambodge* (Manuel d'Archéologie d'Extrême-Orient, 1ère pie: Asie du Sud-Est, I, Paris 1966).

G. Cœdès. *Bronzes khmers* (Ars Asiatica, V, Paris-Bruxelles, 1925).

G. de Coral-Rémusat. *L'art khmer, les grandes étapes de son évolution* (2e édition, Paris, 1951).

P. Dupont. *La statuaire préangkorienne* (Artibus Asiae, Supplementum, Ascona, 1955).

M. Giteau. *Khmer Sculpture and the Angkor Civilization* (New York, 1965).

M. Glaize. *Les Monuments du Groupe d'Angkor. Guide* (3e édition, Paris, 1964).

B.-Ph. Groslier. *Angkor. Hommes et pierres* (Paris, 1956).

L. de Lajonquière. *Inventaire descriptif des Monuments du Cambodge* (Publications E.F.E.O., 3 volumes, 1902–1911).

Sherman E. Lee. *Ancient Cambodian Sculptures* (The Asia Society, 1969).

H. Marchal. *Le décor et la statuaire khmers* (Paris, 1951).

H. Parmentier. *L'art khmer primitif* (Publications E.F.E.O., 1927).

——. *L'art khmer classique. Monuments du quadrant Nord-Est* (Publications E.F.E.O., 1939).

Ph. Stern. *Le Bayon d'Angkor et l'évolution de l'art khmer* (Publications du Musée Guimet, 1927).

——. *Les monuments khmers du style du Bayon et Jayavarman VII* (Publications du Musée Guimet, 1965).

The Chronology

Khmer styles are named after similarly called monuments selected for the characteristics of their essentially architectural sculpture. The overlapping of contiguous styles happens quite frequently.

Periods and Styles	Major Monuments, Constructions, and Artistic Expressions	Major Events	The Kings
Funan Period	3th-4th cent.: Oc-èo: jewels, seals, amulets (of Indian origin, and some of Mediterranean). No known monuments; some questionable vestiges of constructions.	ca. 225: Embassy in India. ca. 231 and later: Embassies in China. Capital at Angkor Borei (?) Buddhist prominence. Relations with China. First Vishnuite inscriptions. Capital at Vyādhapura.	ca. 1st century AD, more or less mythical reign of Kaundinya. Beginning of 3rd cent. reign of Fan Shiman, conqueror, "the great King of Funan." ca. 357: reign of "the Indian Zhantan (Chandan)." ca. 450: first mentions of Zhenla. 478–514: reign of Kaundinya-Jayavarman. 514–after 539: Rudravarman.
Zhenla Period **Pre-Angkorian Period**		After 550: Rise of Zhenla.	
Phnom Dà style 540 (?)–ca. 600 (?)	Only statues are attributed to this style.		
Sambor Prei Kuk style after 600–ca. 650	Numerous temples and shrines at Sambor Prei Kuk, in the Great Lakes region and along the Mekong; Wat Phu (the early part); abundant statuary (mostly Brahmanic).	611–613—First inscriptions in Khmer; Īśānapura, the capital, is located at Sambor Prei Kuk.	Before 615–after 635 Īśānavarman I
Prei Kmeng style 635–after 700		Brahmanic predominance.	645–681 Jayavarman I

Style / Period	Monuments	Historical Events	Reigns
Art of Prasat Andèt ca. 690–after 700	Prei Kmeng (W of Angkor). Prasat Andèt (WSW of Sambor Prei Kuk).		
Kompong Prah style ca. 706–after 800(?)	Prasat Phum Prasat (706 A.D.). Prasat Kompong Prah. 8th cent.: Oc-èo: numerous jewels of gold, pewter from the Mae Nam Basin. Monuments in the Rolùoh region.	713: Partitioning of Zhenla. After 717: Land- (or Upper) Zhenla[1] and Water- (or Lower) Zhenla.[2] ca. 775: probable Indonesian incursions.	
Transition Period			
Kulèn style ca. 825–ca. 875	At Mahendraparvata (present-day Phnom Kulèn): Pr. Damrei Krap, Pr. O Pong, Pr. Neak Ta, Pr. Thmà Dap, Rup Arak, etc. In the Rolùoh region: Pr. Trapeang Phong (main shrine).	Jayavarman II initiated the Śivaite Devarāja cult on Mahendraparvata, and declared the Khmer kingdom secure from Java.	802–850 Jayavarman II 850–877 Jayavarman III
Angkorian Period			
Prah Kô style ca. 877–ca. 893	877: Artificial Sacred Pond Indratatāka at Hariharālaya. 879: Prah Kô (for the benefit of ancestors and predecessors). 881: Bàkong, royal temple. 893: Lolei (built in the center of the Indratatāka), temple for ancestors and predecessors of Yaśovarman I.	Capital at Hariharālaya. First large architectural group (Sacred Pond, ancestral temple, Royal Temple).	877–889 Indravarman I
Bàkheng style after 893–ca. 927	Sacred Pond Yaśodharatatāka (Eastern Bàrai of Angkor) and rectification of the River's course. Śivaite rupestral institutions on Phnom Kulèn. Pr. Phnom Bàkheng (Royal Temple); Pr. Phnom Bok, East of Angkor; Pr. Phnom Krom, S. of Angkor. 921: Pr. Kravan, Angkor. 922: construction of Baksei Chamkrong.	Capital established at Yaśodharapura (the first Angkor centered on the Phnom Bàkheng temple). First monuments built entirely in stone.	893–ca. 900 Yaśovarman I ca. 900–922 Harshavarman

Koh Ker style 921–ca. 945	Prasat Thom at Koh Ker and monuments of the Koh Ker group (Pr. Damrei, Pr. Chrap, Pr. Chen, etc.).	In 921 Jayavarman IV moved the capital to Chok Gargyar (present-day Koh Ker). His reign became legitimized in 928 after the death of Īśānavarman II.	922–927 Īśānavarman II (921) 928–941 Jayavarman IV 941–944 Harshavarman II
Pré Rup style 947–ca. 965	947: Improvements of Baksei Chamkrong. 952: Eastern Mébon temple. 961: Pré Rup. The Royal Palace of Angkor (the beginning of). 946: Pr. Beng Vien. 953: Pr. Bat Chum. } (Buddhist temples). Provincial institutions (Sambor Prei Kuk, etc.).	Return of the capital to Angkor. At Pré Rup linkage of Angkorian monarchy to Bhadreśvara (Wat Phu) the patron deity of the Kambujas. Increased power of the dignitaries. Buddhist renaissance (Tantric Mahāyāna). ca. 950: victorious war against Champa.	944–968 Rājendravarman II
Banteay Srei style 967–ca. 1000 (this style had only a limited spread)	Banteay Srei. Pr. Sralao. Small prasat behind Pr. Khleang north.	967: Śivaite temple (Banteay Srei) endowed by Yajñavarāha, learned dignitary and guru of the King	968–1001 Jayavarman V 1001–1002 Udayādityavarman
Style of the Khleangs ca. 965–1010	Outside walls and gopuras of the Royal Palace of Angkor, Phimeanakas, North Khleang } South Khleang ca. 1002–1010 (?) Pr. Tà Kev (incomplete). Buddhist Cetiyas (votive monuments) at Phnom Srok, etc.	After 1002 war of succession between Jayavīravarman, the usurper, and Sūryavarman I, the rightful pretender. Continued Buddhist revival.	1002–1011 Jayavīravarman (usurper)

Style	Monuments / art	Historical events	Dates and rulers
		Civil servants' oath engraved in Angkor and other high places in the kingdom. 1022–1025: Sūryavarman I conquers the Lopburi region.	1002–1050 Sūryavarman I
Baphûon style ca. 1010–ca. 1080	1018 and after: Pr. Prah Vihear in the Dang Rèk, magic substitute of the Wat Phu Bhadreśvara, Pr. Phnom Chisor, Vat Ek, Vat Baset. Rupestral Vishnuite and Śivaite sculptures on Mt. Kulèn. Sacred Pond west of Angkor, and Pr. Eastern Mébon (Vishnuite), the Baphûon in Angkor, Pr. Khna Sen Kev (northeastern province).	1051: General Sangrāma represses a rebellion in the south, then in 1055 in the NW and in the East. Unsuccessful war against Champa.	1050–1065 Udayādityavarman I
Art of transition and evolution of original architecture and sculpture N. of the Dang Rèk	1080 and after: Pr. Hin Phimai, Mahāyānist center; Pr. Ta Mien Thom, Pr. Phanom Rung, etc., } N. of the Dang Rèk Lack of noteworthy activity in the Angkor region.	1080 and after: advent of the new Mahīdharapura dynasty. Instability in the Angkor region (cf. Epigraphy, p. 117).	1080–1107 Jayavarman VI
		Restoration of Angkorian power; expansion to the NW beyond Lopburi (Sukhothai region), but defeat inflicted by the Môn kingdom of Haripuñjaya (Lamphun). 1128, 1132, 1138: engagements against the Đai Viêt; 1145–1149: engagements against Champa, and partial occupation of that kingdom.	1107–1113 Dharanīdravarman 1113–ca. 1150 Sūryavarman II
Angkor Vat style ca. 1100–ca. 1175	Angkor Vat (Vishnuite temple). Chau Say Tevoda, Thommanon, Vat Athvea, } Angkor region Banteay Samrè, Beng Mealea (ENE of Angkor). Institutions at Wat Phu and Prah Vihear. Central part of Prah Khan of Kompong Svay.	Usurpation and reign of Tribhuvanādityavarman; 1177: capture and occupation of Angkor by the Chams, death of Tribhuvanādityavarman. 1177–1181: War of Liberation waged by the future Jayavarman VII.	1150–1165 Yaśovarman II 1165–1177 Tribhuvanādityavarman

Bàyon style
ca. 1180–ca. 1230

1181–ca. 1218 (?)
Jayavarman VII

Founding of the New Yaśodharapura (Angkor Thom).
Buddhist preponderance (Mahāyāna).
Restoration of Angkorian power.
1190–1203: War against Champa.
1203–1220: Annexation of Champa.
Expansion into the Mae Nam Basin and the Mekong valley (Vientiane).

After 1220: end of Khmer expansion and of the great construction programs.
Liberation of the Mae Nam Thais, birth of the Sukhothai kingdom.

1296–1297: Zhou Daguan accompanied the Chinese (Mongolian) mission to Angkor and gave a description of the capital.
In the early XIVth century: advance of the Theravādin Buddhism, using the Pāli language.
ca. 1353–1358: Occupation of Angkor by the armies of Siam (Ayuthya).
ca. 1369: further occupation of Angkor.
1393–1394: Withdrawal of the court to Basan.
1431: Final capture of Angkor, and coronation of the Ayuthya royal heir.
Further withdrawal to Basan.

Prah Khan of Kompong Svay and monuments of that group.
Outer wall with five monumental gates of Angkor Thom and the Bàyon temple; Banteay Kdei;
1186: Tà Prohm of Angkor;
1191: Prah Khan of Angkor (complex with Sacred Pond, Neak Pean, etc.).
In the provinces: West: Banteay Chmar; South: Ta Prohm of Bàti; Southeast: Vat Nokor, etc.
Construction of cities and monuments in the Mae Nam Basin: Phimai, Muang Singh, etc., and in Champa.
Originality and abundance of statuary.
Road constructions with stone bridges, hospitals, and edifices known as "dharmaśālās" throughout the empire.

Post Angkorian period			
ca. mid-16th cent., in Angkor: completion of the bas-reliefs of the Angkor Vat gallery; work done on the Royal Terraces of Angkor Thom, etc. In the provinces, work done at Vat Nokor, among others. 1586: Prah Thom, great rupestral Buddha on Phnom Kulên. Rupestral institutions on Phnom Santŭk. Increased use of wood in sculpture.	The capital is established at Cadomukh (also known as "The Four Arms," future Phnom Penh). Reorganization of the kingdom. 1528: the capital is established at Lovêk. ca. 1546–1597: temporary reclaiming of Angkor.	1504–1566 Ang Chan	
		1566–1576 Paramarāja I	
		1576–1594 Sotha I	
	1594: Conquest of Lovêk by King Prah Nareth of Ayuthya. Flight of King Sotha I to Laos.		

---

[1]Land- (or Upper) Zhenla: between the middle course of the Mekong and the river Mun.
[2]Water- (or Lower) Zhenla: Southern Cambodia South of the Great Lakes.

www.ingramcontent.com/pod-product-compliance
Lightning Source LLC
Chambersburg PA
CBHW081003170526
45158CB00010B/2885